D0848182

A Guide to Effective Sermon Delivery

A Guide to Effective Sermon Delivery

by
Jerry Vines

MOODY PRESS
CHICAGO

ISBN: 0-8024-4896-8

1 2 3 4 5 6 7 Printing/AF/Year 90 89 88 87 86

Printed in the United States of America

Contents

Foreword

There is a distinct difference between speaking and preaching. This book deals with the preaching. If the church in America is once again to become a dynamic, moving force for righteousness in our society, then its pulpits must be filled with godly men of courage committed to the Book and skilled in persuasively delivering their message from God.

I believe this book can become a powerful tool in the improvement of the preacher's sermon delivery. It will prove extremely helpful to those who have been trained in sermon delivery and to those who have not.

In the very first section Dr. Vines deals with a vital area of sermon delivery most preachers ignore until they are forced to face it because of health reasons—the proper use and care of the voice. He speaks from the experience of his own problems in this area and offers excellent and practical advice that will prove profitable to everyone who studies it.

Much preaching today leaves people with the feeling, "So what?" They listen to a sermon but go away without being persuaded to do anything about what they have heard. The author says, "Persuasion is what preaching is all about. The whole existence and purpose of the sermon is in order to persuade. It moves the souls of men." He illustrates the wrong and the right way to persuade an audience. The study of this section will help to put "punch" into your delivery.

The key to effective preaching is total dependence upon the

Holy Spirit in both the preparation and the proclamation of the message. What the Holy Spirit burns into the heart of the preacher He can most effectively proclaim through the heart of the preacher. Dr. Vines illustrates this truth in a manner you will find both helpful and convicting.

For you men of God who want to reach the maximum of your potential in the proclamation of the gospel of Jesus Christ, study this book prayerfully.

Dr. Charles F. Stanley
Pastor, First Baptist Church of Atlanta
President, Southern Baptist Convention

Acknowledgments

I would like to express gratitude to several people who have been instrumental in the writing of this book: Dr. Paige Patterson, who urged me on in its inception and completion; Mrs. Shirley Cannon, who worked very hard preparing the manuscript; Dr. Homer Lindsay, Jr., my partner in ministry; our dear people of First Baptist Church, Jacksonville, Florida; my wife, Janet, and our children—Joy, Jodi, Jim, Jon—the dearest family any preacher could ever have.

Introduction

The words hit me like a laser beam. "You will have to be completely silent for the next two weeks. You have a nodule on the anterior third of your right vocal cord. Surgery is the only way to remove it. I'm not sure when you will be back in the pulpit. Perhaps ninety days or longer."

For several years I had experienced some degree of hoarseness. I had never thought much about it. But for several weeks the hoarseness had become rather pronounced and persistent. I could not finish a sermon without getting so hoarse I could hardly speak above a whisper. In the morning in normal conversation I found myself getting hoarse, so I went to a throat specialist.

I was totally unprepared for what he said. The thought of surgery on my vocal cords frightened me. I could hear the voices of several older preachers I knew who had had throat surgery several times. I did not want my voice to sound that way. Would the surgery be effective? How long would I be out of the pulpit?

The days ahead were emotional and traumatic. I really didn't know what to do. A member in my congregation recommended that I contact Dr. Stephen Olford, who had experienced similar difficulties. Dr. Olford gave me the name of Dr. Friedrich Brodnitz, a throat specialist in New York City. Dr. Brodnitz confirmed that I did have a vocal nodule, but he did not recommend surgery. He said that surgery would remove the nodule only for a while. I must correct the habits that had produced the nodule. If

I didn't start speaking differently, another nodule would form. He recommended that I return home and find a competent speech pathologist.

That is exactly what I did. Dr. Sam Faircloth, a speech pathologist in Mobile, Alabama, helped me determine the abuses that had created the nodule in the first place. When those abuses were corrected the nodule disappeared within a matter of weeks! No surgery. From that day until now I have had no recurrence of the problem.

What seemed to have been the worst thing that ever happened to me actually was one of the greatest blessings to come my way. I am able to preach several times every day without strain. Unless I have a cold or some problem with allergy, I never experience hoarseness. In the course of my own recovery from vocal problems I became much interested in the subject of speech itself. Reading books on speech almost became a hobby for me. The result is the book in your hands.

Why am I writing a book on sermon delivery? What qualifies me to do so? I am genuinely interested in helping my preacher brethren learn to be more effective in the delivery of their sermons. I believe this book can help any preacher be a better pulpit communicator. My primary qualification for writing is that I am a preacher. I preach many, many times each week. My life is spent either in the pulpit or preparing for the pulpit. The contents of this book have been hammered out in my own ministry. This does not mean that I perfectly demonstrate what sermon delivery ought to be. I am still in the process of learning. I work every day on improving my delivery. Actually, writing this book has helped me in several areas of my own delivery.

Throat difficulties affect everyone who uses his voice in his work. The "preacher's throat" is almost proverbial. There may be a variety of reasons preachers are vulnerable. The tensions of modern life attack the preacher as well as others in our fast-paced society. The preacher is susceptible to the same allergies others have. If he does not understand how to use his voice correctly, vocal abuse can create nagging throat problems.

The Inner Struggle

The preacher may face another tension. Within us there is an emotional struggle. The preaching of the gospel of Jesus Christ is the most real, vital part of our lives. Deep within are feelings of love, gratitude, and longing for the Lord Jesus and for those who need to know Him. Those emotions must be expressed as we preach. But how does the preacher express the depths of his feeling without abusing the voice?

This is especially a problem for those of us who have been brought up in the South. Where we live, there is a difference between preaching and just talking. The preacher's verse in my part of the woods is: "Cry aloud and spare not." No sincere preacher from the South wants to be a dry, lifeless preacher. In Georgia, my home state, if you could speak above a whisper on Monday morning, you had compromised on Sunday! Preaching in the South is an all-out, heartfelt, top-of-your-voice affair.

John Broadus summarizes the cultural situation quite well:

> It was speaking long on a high key in the open air, with unrestrained passion, that led many of the early Baptist preachers of this country into that singsong, or "holy whine," which is still heard in some parts of the country. The voice, strained and fatigued, instinctively sought relief in a rhythmical rise and fall, as is also the case in the loud cries of street peddlers. They were commonly zealous and sometimes great men who fell into this fault, and it was often imitated by those who followed them, after the usual superficial fashion of imitators, mistaking the obvious fault for the hidden power. To some. . .this particular whine is connected by a lifelong association with the most impressive truths and most solemn occasions; and so it touches their feelings, independently of what is said, and sometimes when the preacher's words are not heard—like the revival tunes. . .familiar to us from childhood.[1]

Such cultural characteristics also bring the opposite reaction. Because some preachers are overzealous and too emotional

1. John A. Broadus, *The Preparation and Delivery of Sermons* (New York: Harper, 1926), p. 346.

in their delivery, men who do not want to be identified with such fervor tend to go to the opposite extreme. Any expression of feeling or fervor in pulpit delivery is looked down upon. The approach is to present the sermon in an inanimate, unemotional, matter-of-fact manner. This extreme is just as detrimental in preaching the Word as the other—perhaps more so.

But back to the inner struggle. As I abused my voice in preaching, a question kept nagging me. If I am preaching in the power of the Holy Spirit, why, then, is the Holy Spirit abusing His own temple? Am I relying on the Holy Spirit or on my own abilities and efforts?

I have good news for you. You can express the deepest feelings of your faith and your ministry with power and fervor without abusing your voice. Understanding the aspects of sermon delivery in this book will enable you to preach with all the fervor of your soul and still maintain a healthy voice.

Marketing Your Sermon

Sermon delivery is an important aspect of the preacher's work. At this point many preachers fail. They may gather excellent material for their sermons. The sermon itself may be well organized and skillfully done. Yet when the preacher opens his mouth in the pulpit, the sermon dies. There is no positive, enthusiastic response. This must be corrected. The preacher must not only prepare his sermons well, he must also deliver them well.

I call this the marketing aspect of the preaching enterprise. Preparing the sermon is in the realm of manufacturing. Sermon preparation gets the content together. But the product is not in the hands of the people until we market it. This book centers on marketing—how to deliver the content effectively and attractively to people.

Most preachers can get the content. Colleges and seminaries normally do a commendable job in this area. But little training is provided in how to deliver the message utilizing the various techniques of effective speech communication. This lack of training is painfully apparent. Much preaching today is accurately described by Spurgeon as "Articulate snoring."[2]

2. In John R.W. Stott, *Between Two Worlds* (Grand Rapids: Eerdmans, 1982), p. 275.

The importance of an effective delivery is considerable. Think of the hours of time involved when the preacher stands to deliver his sermon. Dr. Paige Patterson tells his homiletics students that the preacher uses or abuses more corporate hours than any other single individual in our society; the preacher who preaches weekly to one thousand members for forty years will use time equal to 3,120,000 man hours.

The great preachers have been known for the effectiveness of their delivery. Contemporary preachers who are really listened to are men who are masters in sermon delivery. They are, in the finest sense of the term, pulpit communicators. My desire is to help you become effective in communicating the Word of God to people.

Five aspects of effective sermon delivery form the basis of this book. First is a section about mechanical aspects of delivery, including a simple discussion of the essential ingredients of effective vocal production. The second section discusses the mental aspects of delivery. My purpose is to show how the mental images that form the basis of your words can be strengthened to make your speaking more effective. The third section is a discussion of the rhetorical aspects of effective delivery—how to use words effectively, persuasively, and with oratorical power. The psychological aspects of effective sermon delivery is the fourth section. I want to show you how to utilize sound principles of psychology in your sermon delivery.

The final section I consider to be the most vital. A knowledge of all the other elements of effective speech communication will never make you an effective preacher. The spiritual dimension is what transforms one from merely a speaker to a preacher aflame for God.

Your voice is a divinely prepared instrument for conveying the Word of God. I hope this book will give you the beginning steps in learning how to "lift up your voice" (cf. Isa. 58:1).

PART I

Mechanical Aspects of Sermon Delivery

God has prepared a marvelous instrument with which you may convey His Word to men. Some have referred to the voice as the queen of the instruments. It has the clarity of the trumpet, the brilliance of the violin, and the melody of the oboe. The voice is unsurpassed in its ability to express with depth and meaning the intended message of its user. This brilliant instrument is the common property of every person. The words people use every day are colored with its emotional undertones, its energy, and its powers of persuasion.

The Vocal Mechanism

Yet though each of us uses his voice daily, the average person knows little about his vocal mechanism. That may be acceptable in persons who are not professional speakers, but it is not in a person who uses his voice professionally. Those persons should know something about the nature and function of the vocal mechanism. This is especially true of the preacher. The man whom God has called to preach is assigned to communicate the eternal Word of God in his own words. Those words are produced by a complex vocal mechanism. For this reason the preacher's voice may be considered his God-given tool. A great deal of the effectiveness of his message depends upon the manner in which he handles that mechanism. Also, knowing more about his voice will assist him in guarding its health.

How much do you know about your vocal mechanism? If I should ask you about the location of the vocal cords, what would you say? Are your vocal cords suspended vertically or horizontally? Few preachers really know much about the structure and function of the vocal mechanism. Most preachers are taught the basic techniques of speech, but few understand the nature of their vocal mechanism, how to effectively employ it, and how to adequately care for it.

Some object that too much knowledge about the vocal mechanism may upset the balance that is intuitive in the speaking process. That fear is unfounded. To be sure, we must not allow ourselves to become so occupied with mechanics of delivery that the tool becomes a hindrance rather than a help. But any person can use a tool more effectively if he understands how the tool is designed. The baseball pitcher can become even more effective when he learns as much as possible about his pitching arm, the baseball, and the factors that make for good delivery. The same is true of the preacher and a knowledge of his voice.

In this section I will discuss the basic aspects of the vocal mechanism. Probably you can name most of the organs involved. You have a nose, throat, voice box, vocal cords, windpipe, and lungs. You also have a diaphragm, sinuses, and many muscles related to the throat, voice box, and chest cavities. Rather interestingly, the same organs for speech are also the organs for breathing. Some, who hold to the evolutionary view, theorize that speaking came as an incidental result of the intended function of breathing. Those of us who hold to the creation model to explain man's existence do not share this view. The faculty for speech is a divinely designed function that makes possible man's communication with his fellowman. To observe the dual functions of speaking and breathing is a fascinating study.

A Tour of the Vocal Organs

Come with me on an imaginary tour through the vocal organs. To do this we will trace the course of air through all those parts of the body that make up the channel of inhaled air.

These are the nose, throat, voice box, windpipe, bronchi, and lungs.

Air enters your body in one of two ways. As you are sitting quietly reading this book, your mouth is probably closed and you are inhaling through your nose. The air comes through your nose by means of the nostrils and travels through the nasal cavity to the throat.

Air may also come into the body through the mouth. For instance, when we are speaking we bring air into our bodies through the mouth as well as the nose. Just a few matters relating to the voice and the mouth should be noted. The tongue is a part of the mouth, and it is much larger than you might suppose. Actually, most of your mouth is filled with your tongue. Do not be offended when I say that your tongue is the biggest thing in your mouth! The air moves gently over your tongue down into the throat. In the back of your mouth cavity you also have adenoids. They form a cushion behind your soft palate. On each side of your tongue are tonsils. You may or may not still have them. If infected, your tonsils can become greatly swollen and hinder the free use of your voice.

When air leaves your nose or mouth and goes to the throat it enters the respiratory tract. The air goes from there into the windpipe.

Next we find ourselves in the chest. Air passes into the chest by means of pipelines called *bronchi*. You have two bronchi for each lung. The air flows through the bronchi into the lobes of the lungs. The lungs fill most of your chest. Room is left for your heart and the esophagus. The chest cavity is actually a cage formed by your breastbone, ribs, and the spinal column. When air is pushed from the lungs through the pressure of the diaphragm, the process is called exhalation.

The air leaves the lungs by means of exhalation and passes through the bronchi and the windpipe until it arrives at the voice box. The proper name for the voice box is the *larynx*. The larynx is a remarkably complex organ. The method of suspension used in its construction anticipates the use of springs in much of our current technical design. The larynx consists of several muscles and cartilages. We will not go into detail concerning each part.

Our primary interest is in the vocal cords. Most prefer to call them vocal folds. They are actually folds of muscle tissue suspended horizontally in the larynx. The two vocal folds are attached in front of the voice box to the thyroid cartilage. These folds, like wings, meet at the front of the throat. They always touch each other at that point. In the rear of the voice box the folds are connected to muscles that make it possible for them to be opened and closed. Normally the folds are whitish in color, although some are more pinkish-gray. This is especially true with those who have deeper voices. Normal folds have a smooth, glistening surface. They are covered above with folds of mucous membrane called false cords or folds.

Sound is produced when the folds are brought together and air pushes through them. Contraction of the muscles in the vocal folds makes them thicker, shorter, or more tense. This tensing of the vocal folds makes speech possible. When air blows through the vocal folds the resulting sound is call *phonation.* This sound is carried through the throat into the mouth cavity. At this point the sound is amplified by the cavities of the mouth and nose and throat. The amplification of sound is called *resonation.* The human voice is unique because its resonating cavities can be partly altered. Only the nose is a rigid, unalterable structure. The throat, mouth, tongue, and lips can all be changed by muscular action.[1] Those actions form the sound that has been produced into words. Thus, the process of speech—"voice or voiceless breath, modified by articulation—has occurred."[2]

The chapters that follow give the essential ingredients of the mechanical aspects of delivery. An understanding of those mechanical factors will prepare you to use your God-given voice to its fullest potential.

Chapter 1 has to do with the importance of relaxation. Preachers are involved in high-tension areas of work. Learning to relax the body and vocal mechanism is crucial to their achieving good mechanical delivery.

1. Friedrich Brodnitz, *Keep Your Voice Healthy* (Springfield, Ill.: Thomas, 1973), p. 36.
2. Ibid., p. 45.

The next two chapters discuss two aspects of vocal production essential to relaxed speaking—in Chapter 2, proper breathing; in chapter 3, proper articulation. In both chapters exercises are given to assist the speaker in improving in those areas.

Chapter 4 discusses integrating the various factors of good vocal production, such as rate, volume, phrasing, and pause. Chapter 5 suggests how the speaker can learn to do a better job of using the vocal mechanism and will help him avoid some pitfalls that are often encountered in learning to use the voice properly.

Chapter 6 discusses preserving the speaking voice. Most preachers have a tendency to abuse their voices and therefore suffer from a variety of vocal disorders. Some of those disorders can be prevented if proper care is given to the voice.

All of the chapters in this section are intended to help you begin doing a better job of using your voice effectively.

1

Relaxing

We are living in tension-filled times. Perhaps more people are under pressure than ever before. The advent of our modern conveniences and advantages has also brought with it definite liabilities. The average person works more hours than he previously did. Battling traffic to and from work increases the tension level. Pressure to succeed and produce in the marketplace has greatly increased the level of stress. Ours is a day of the heart attack and high blood pressure. The ulcer has almost become a status symbol of our times.

More and more industries are recognizing the necessity of proper relaxation on the part of their workers. Overall productivity is increased when industries assist their personnel in alleviating as much job tension as possible. All across the country much emphasis is being placed upon proper exercise, coping with stress, and quality leisure time.

Preacher Tensions

The preacher does not escape the tensions of the times. The average pastor experiences as many or even more tensions than do his people. There are the normal struggles he experiences as a member of a complex society: the stress of making a living; the pressure of providing adequately for his family; the constant push to see that his church grows.

In addition, the preacher faces other complications. The man of God studies his New Testament and sees clearly what God expects the church to be. The level of expectation for the individual Christian in the New Testament is clearly discernible as well. On the other hand, the preacher sees his church as it actually is. More than anyone else he is keenly aware of its—and his own—failures and shortcomings. The level of living he observes in the lives of his people too often is far below the New Testament standard. Thus the preacher encounters the disparity between the ideal and the real. These pressure points can create tremendous frustration and anxiety.

What does all this have to do with the mechanics of vocal production? Much in every way. I encountered problems with my voice during the most difficult pastorate in my ministry. Prior to that time my experiences with congregations had been most pleasant and congenial. But in that particular pastorate I found myself in the midst of a people with unusual spiritual problems. There was much animosity among the members. I inherited a church staff where there was bickering, jealousy, and carnality. Almost every ministry of the church was in jeopardy. Preaching in this atmosphere brought tremendous physical tension upon me. Although initially I was unaware of the situation, eventually vocal difficulties made it apparent to me that the tensions of the pastorate were affecting my vocal delivery.

Moreover, the church auditorium was a speaker's nightmare. There was almost no way to get adequate sound in the building. Designed for architectural beauty rather than speaking and hearing ease, the building was acoustically inadequate. There were three echo chambers in the building. Because of a horseshoe balcony there were massive pillars in the building. Such poor physical facilities increased the difficulty of speaking, thereby further increasing my tension. Looking back upon the experience, I can see my vocal difficulties were inevitable.

A man's tension goes to his job. The accountant battles tension headaches. The baseball pitcher struggles with a sore arm. The preacher grapples with throat problems. Undue tension makes it difficult to adequately perform. The pianist with taut fingers cannot play creditably. The artist with tense hands cannot paint as he desires. Neither can the preacher who has undue tension expect to speak with a clear, positive, pleasant voice. There are many signs of undue tension. An uncomfortable nervousness, inadequate breathing habits, a jerky rhythm in speaking, an unusually fast delivery—all these may indicate the preacher is experiencing excessive tension.[1] The preacher who is speaking with ease and in a relaxed condition will indicate the same in the vitality and quality of his speaking voice.

The total personality of the preacher will affect his voice. If you are tense vocally, chances are you are tense in many other ways. You should make careful evaluation of the causes of that tension. Take a good look at the circumstances of your life. Honestly face your negative attitudes and unspoken fears. Evaluate your attitude toward the pastorate where you serve. Evaluate your own inner tensions. You may need to reorganize your thinking and develop new methods of coping with your personal and pastoral difficulties. That may be the first step in learning to speak in a relaxed manner. Without relaxation the voice cannot be well coordinated, free in its function, and vibrant in its expression.

Proper relaxation is the first step in developing a well coordinated voice. The muscles in your face, tongue, jaw, chin, throat, and neck affect the muscles that control your vocal folds. Unless you accomplish muscular freedom, your speaking will be tension-bound.[2]

Dr. Friedrich Brodnitz, an authority on the proper use and care of the voice, maintains that most voice troubles result from exaggerated muscle activity. In order to correct this, the hyperfunction of the muscles that relate to the vocal mechanism must be reduced.[3] The latter part of this chapter will give some helpful exercises to reduce tension in those muscles, for if the muscles of the throat and mouth are too tense, the vocal mechanism will be cramped. The result will be poor speaking quality. The voice will sound as strained as it is. In addition to a poor, unpleasant sound, health problems will inevitably result. There will be a tendency to place the voice in a wrong pitch. There will also be a

1. Dorothy Mulgrave, *Speech* (New York: Barnes and Noble, 1954), p. 162.
2. David Blair McClosky, *Your Voice at Its Best* (Plymouth, Mass.: Memorial, 1972), p. 4.
3. Friedrich Brodnitz, *Keep Your Voice Healthy* (Springfield, Ill.: Thomas, 1973), p. 191.

tendency to speak louder in order to overcome the lack of sound such a restricted mechanism produces.

Let me hasten to say that we do not want total relaxation of all muscles related to vocal production. Using the vocal mechanism for speech is an active function of the body. Any action of body muscles is dependent upon some degree of tension. Physiologists call this muscle tonus. Every biological function is dependent upon a proper balance between tension and relaxation. The vocal mechanism depends on use of the right muscles and the application of a proper degree of muscle tonus.

Vocal Muscles

The muscles of the voice box are in two general groups. Some of the muscles are located inside the larynx. They directly control the vocal folds. They move the larynx and enable it to function. These muscles are called the *intrinsic muscles.* We need not concern ourselves about manipulating them, for merely thinking of speaking alters them to their task. They operate without conscious thought.

The second group of muscles is called the *extrinsic muscles.* They are on the outside of the vocal mechanism, around the throat. If the extrinsic muscles are unduly tense, the intrinsic muscles cannot function properly. Our purpose is to relax this outer set of muscles enough to allow the inner muscles to function without being in a cramped position. The goal is well-summarized by Dwight E. Stevenson and Charles F. Diehl: "Speech. . . is not complete relaxation, but tonus. Tonus is that delicate balance of tension and relaxation—neither too much nor too little—appropriate for what has to be done."[4]

Learning to Relax

There are ways to eliminate muscle tension before you speak. Let me walk you through a series of procedures that will

---

4. Dwight E. Stevenson and Charles F. Diehl, *Reaching People from the Pulpit* (Grand Rapids: Baker, 1958), p. 44.

help you to be relaxed when you preach. Here are some suggestions that have been helpful to me.

Begin your preparation for speaking before you leave home. Try this approach—but in privacy. An observer might think you're crazy! Begin by lying down flat on your back. You can lie on the bed, if you desire. I prefer to lie upon the floor. Completely stretch out your arms and your legs. Tense your whole body. Hold the tension until you feel your muscles beginning to quiver. Then, with a sigh, release the tension. Allow every part of your body to slump in exhaustion. Next, tense the muscles of your legs until they quiver. Release the tension. Then, tense your arms until they quiver. Release them. Tense your facial and throat muscles. Release them. Tense the muscles of your abdomen, chest, shoulders, and neck. Release them. At this point, glance around the room to be sure no one is present! Begin to talk softly to your body. Begin with your feet. As you gradually move your feet at the ankles, tell your feet to relax. Repeat the process with your legs, bending them at the knees and hips. Move to your arms. Turn your wrists, move your elbows and your shoulders, talking to them all the while in soothing tones. Then gradually move your head from side to side. With a big sigh tell your body to take it easy. If you are not careful, you may go back to sleep and be late for the preaching service.

Select a shirt with a loose collar. I call these my preaching collars. Keep in mind that the throat has a tendency to enlarge during the heat of delivery. For this reason, your collar should be as loose as possible.

I drive approximately fifteen miles to church. During this drive I engage in several activities to help me prepare my voice. Several times I go over the notes on the musical scale with a soft *ah* sound. This warms up my voice. Many times I do the breathing and articulating drills I will give you in the next two chapters. By the time I arrive at church my voice is warm and ready to go.

If possible, find a quiet place for a few minutes before you are to preach. Perhaps in your study at church you will be able to spend a few uninterrupted moments. Sit in a comfortable position and try to eliminate any disturbing thoughts that might increase your tension. In an unhurried, unpressed manner, do these exercises.

First, starting at the hairline and working down to your lower neck, massage very gently all the muscles of your face and throat. You will be able to feel with your fingers any tension in these muscles. As you stroke these muscles downward let your face become as limp as possible. Move your fingers over your eyes. Close them as you do. Let your jaw hang limp.

When your jaw drops, allow your tongue to come over your lower lip as much as you can. Do not force this. Let it happen naturally.

The swallowing muscles may next be relaxed. Using the fingers of both hands press gently on each side of your throat, beginning at the jaw and moving to the Adam's apple. Massage these muscles very gently. Swallow, and feel how much more relaxed these muscles are. This will greatly reduce tension in your throat.

Next, take your chin in hand and move it up and down, right and left. This will decrease any resistance in your jaw. There is a tendency for the jaw muscles to stiffen when there is too much tension. Work your jaw muscles until they are as relaxed as possible. Take your time.

Now take your voice box between your thumb and fingers on one hand and move it from side to side until it is free of tension.

Make sure the muscles of your neck are relaxed. Allow your head to nod up and down and roll from side to side.[5]

Yawn several times. This will relax all the muscles of the face and throat. When you get ready to go into the pulpit these exercises should make you as tension free as you need to be for effective speaking.

The next two chapters will discuss the role of good breathing and the place of proper articulation in effective vocal delivery. The two activities are also important in maintaining a relaxed throat. Improper breathing and poor articulation greatly increase the tension in one's voice box.

5. McClosky, pp. 6-8.

Read as much as possible about relaxation. There are several good books on the subject. Edmund Jacobson's book, *You Must Relax,* (New York: McGraw-Hill, 1942) is a good one. Learn to relax. This will facilitate your ability to use every aspect of your vocal mechanism correctly.

2

Breathing

Breathing is a rather unusual bodily function in that it is done both unconsciously and consciously. In the normal course of our daily activities we do not consciously tell our bodies to breathe. During most normal conversation we do not have to instruct our lungs to supply the necessary air. For speaking or preaching, however, breathing must be consciously controlled. The key to a smoothly functioning vocal mechanism is proper breathing.

When we are not consciously speaking or thinking about breathing, our body provides enough air to do everything we need to do. Whether we are running or are climbing up a steep hill, our body gives us the air we need. As soon as we begin to speak, though, a different kind of breathing must begin. We must see to it that we have sufficient breath to complete our sentences without gulping or losing the closing words. In addition, we must have enough air and control of that air to sustain and, if necessary, amplify our voices during the sentence. This air supply must be taken in and expelled without disturbing our flow of speech. We must gradually propel our breath in a relaxed manner, completing each statement in the most effective way possible.

Breathing Correctly

Correct breathing is closely related to speaking with relaxation. To breathe correctly will greatly relieve muscle tension in the throat. If a speaker does not have an ample supply of air, he will find himself squeezing for air at the throat. That can do great damage to his voice.

Jay Adams minimizes the importance of breathing. He says, "Breathing is not a problem at all for most speakers. Shoulder raising habits and exercises in so-called diaphragmatic breathing are useless in improving one's breathing for speech. In the first place, all breathing is diaphragmatic."[1] That is a somewhat simplistic approach. The large number of preachers who encounter difficulties with their voices causes one to question Adams's conclusion. Failure to breathe properly creates several problems for the speaker. There must be a sufficient supply of air if the necessary volume is to be achieved. Proper breathing will also permit him to speak at length before crowds without undue fatigue or an aching throat.[2] The many problems large numbers of preachers have with their voices indicates that we must understand what proper breathing for speaking is.

Actually there are two kinds of breathing, which are very different from one another. There is one kind of breathing for our physical, biological needs and another kind needed for speech. In order to understand proper breathing for speech, let me briefly review the operation of the respiratory system. Respiration provides the power source for speaking. The lungs themselves provide no power of movement, but respond to changes that are made in the size of the chest cavity. During inhalation the muscles of the chest lift the ribs upward and outward away from the lungs. During this motion the diaphragm moves downward from its dome-shaped position. The result of this action is a rush of air from the nose down the windpipe through the bronchi to the lungs. When exhalation occurs, the diaphragm returns to its dome shape. The rib muscles relax themselves and the rib cage returns downward and inward as air is thrust from the lungs.[3]

1. Jay Adams, *Pulpit Speech* (Phillipsburg, N.J.: Presbyterian and Reformed, 1971), p. 131.
2. William G. Hoffman, *How to Make Better Speeches* (New York: Funk & Wagnalls, 1976), p. 174.
3. Judson S. Crandell and Gerald M. Phillips, *Speech: A Course in Fundamentals* (Glenview, Ill.: Scott, Foresman, 1963), p. 35.

Breathing for speaking can be accomplished in two different ways. The diaphragm divides the chest cavity into two main sections, the clavicle area and the abdominal area. The clavicle area is the upper chest. Breathing may be accomplished by pressure from the clavicle area. This breathing is much like that which the athlete does during competition. It expands the upper chest and is relatively short and quick in nature. Such breathing places pressure upon the entire throat area. Tension is created in the throat as well as the voice box. Prolonged speaking using clavicular breathing will give one a constricted tone, a weary sounding throat, and a hoarse voice.[4] Vocal difficulties will be the inevitable result of such breathing.

The best breathing for speaking is abdominal breathing. The earlier writers and voice teachers referred to this as diaphragmatic breathing. Actually that term is somewhat misleading, for all breathing is diaphragmatic. All breathing is not abdominal, however. During expiration the abdominal muscles should do the real work. The slow relaxation of the diaphragm ensures smooth control of expiration, but the conscious control of the abdominal muscles makes this possible. In correct breathing for speaking we must be consciously aware of the action of our abdominal muscles.

You can easily tell if your breathing is clavicular or abdominal. Place your hand upon your upper chest. Inhale and quote John 3:16. If your upper chest expands when you inhale, you are breathing incorrectly. Then place your hand upon your abdomen, inhale, and quote John 3:16. If your abdominal muscles expand, you are breathing correctly. Undue tension in your throat as you exhale will also alert you to improper breathing. If your voice is breathy or weak or has a harsh quality about it, the likelihood is that you are breathing incorrectly. If you are breathing improperly, you need to correct the problem as soon as possible.

I must hasten to say, however, that breathing abdominally does not mean that you must always take long, deep breaths.

4. Dwight E. Stevenson and Charles F. Diehl, *Reaching People from the Pulpit* (Grand Rapids: Baker, 1958), p. 42.

Such deep breathing can cause unnecessary tension in your throat just as much as clavicular breathing. You only need to breath deeply enough to maintain a sufficient amount of air for good speaking and good support. The amount of air that remains in your lungs after you exhale is residual air. The maximum amount of air you can exhale as you speak is the vital capacity available for speaking. You should breathe only deeply enough to complete your sentence with good support and emphasis.

Begin immediately to change your method of breathing for speaking if you have been breathing incorrectly. The new method will seem unnatural to you for a while. As you learn to breathe more deeply, utilizing the abdominal muscles, you may experience some dizziness. That will mean that you have not been fully utilizing your lung capacity. Dizziness will disappear after a few days. As you practice the exercises I give at the end of this chapter you will learn how to breathe correctly.

Good posture is necessary to proper breathing. Stand erect as you practice proper breathing. The concentration of energy should be at your belt line rather than your throat. Practice inhaling quickly and unobtrusively.[5] One of the primary purposes in learning to breathe correctly is to enable you to replenish your air supply quickly, without disturbing your flow of words. Learn to take your deepest breaths between sentences. Along the way you might want to take little "teacup" breaths as well.

Learning to breathe correctly may be somewhat frustrating to you at the beginning. Do your practicing outside the pulpit. When I encountered my own voice difficulties, I was immediately instructed to change my method of breathing in the pulpit. Doing so reminded me of learning to change gears in a car. The experience was a jerky, frustrating one. During your sermon is not the best time to learn to breathe correctly.

Breathing Exercises

Establish your new breathing by means of good breathing exercises. Practice these in your study. Practice them while you

5. Charlotte I. Lee and Frank Galati, *Oral Interpretation* (Boston: Houghton Mifflin, 1977), p. 107.

drive your car. Practice them as you walk on the sidewalk. Use the method of proper breathing when you read aloud from printed material. Do not try to change your method of breathing during your sermon next Sunday! You have enough to think about while you preach without being burdened with a change in your breathing method. As you learn to breathe correctly in other settings your breathing for preaching will automatically be changed.

The exercises below are designed to assist you in controlled breathing for speaking. They will train you to get the most economical use of breath as you speak.

1. Observe good speakers who have adequate vocal power and breath control. Notice the expansion of the lower chest cavity as they inhale. Notice also that the chest cavity decreases gradually and slowly so that a reserve of breath is constantly maintained. This is good supporting of the vocal tone. Also notice that the well-coordinated speaker seems to have a reserve of breath that enables him to release air when he feels the need for emphasis in his utterance.

2. Use a series of simple exercises to develop your own breath as you speak.
   a) Inhale easily as though you are about to speak. Hold the breath inhaled silently for a moment. Imagine you are speaking a simple word or phrase. Release the breath and let the air flow out gradually, without forcing.
   b) Repeat the previous exercise and gradually increase the length of time you can hold the air in without excessive tension or strain. Release the breath.
   c) Repeat the exercise again, and speak a single word or phrase. Be aware of the outer movement of the abdomen during inhalation. Also be aware of the inward movement of the abdomen as you exhale during the speaking of a word or phase.
   d) Inhale a sufficient supply of air. Then exhale using a

single word or vowel such as *ah, oh, e, u.* Maintain
the tone as long as your breath will allow. Stop before
you lose an awareness of a reserve supply of breath in
your lungs.

e) Repeat the exercise. This time speak a series of
numbers such as one, two, three, four, five, in sequence. Continue counting as long as you can maintain a comfortable flow of breath. See how high you
can count on one breath without releasing all your
reserve air. This is merely for the purpose of exercise.
In your speaking you should never try to speak as
much as possible on one breath.

The following exercises were given to me by a speech
pathologist. Learn to read each of them in one breath. Inhale a
sufficient supply of air. Then, maintaining smooth expiration,
read each sentence. As you work on these exercises you will
increase your capacity for adequate breath for speaking.

The House That Jack Built

This is the house that Jack built.//

This is the malt that lay in the house that Jack built.//

This is the rat that ate the malt that lay in the house that Jack
built.//

This is the cat that caught the rat that ate the malt that lay in the
house that Jack built.//

This is the dog that worried the cat that caught the rat that ate the
malt that lay in the house that Jack built.// 10 seconds

This is the cow with the crumpled horn that tossed the dog that
worried the cat that caught the rat that ate the malt that lay in the
house that Jack built.// 12 seconds

This is the maiden all forlorn that milked the cow with the crumpled horn that tossed the dog that worried the cat that caught the rat that ate the malt that lay in the house that Jack built.// 15 seconds

This is the man all tattered and torn who kissed the maiden all forlorn that milked the cow with the crumpled horn that tossed the dog that worried the cat that caught the rat that ate the malt that lay in the house that Jack built.// 17 seconds

This is the priest all shaven and shorn that married the man all tattered and torn who kissed the maiden all forlorn that milked the cow with the crumpled horn that tossed the dog that worried the cat that caught the rat that ate the malt that lay in the house that Jack built.// 20 seconds

These exercises are designed to help you learn how to breathe correctly. They are also intended to teach you to maintain good breath control during speaking. Also, you will learn how to maintain an adequate reserve supply of breath.

Breathing correctly will help you maintain a good, strong vocal mechanism. Everything that follows is dependent upon learning to breathe correctly. Do not expect to be able to breathe correctly after going over these exercises a few times. Very often good breathing habits must be developed over a long period of time. These exercises should be practiced daily until proper breathing for speaking is as natural to you as normal breathing is for living.

3

Articulating

There are four facets in the process of producing sound for speaking: breathing, phonating, resonating, and articulating. In the previous chapter we discussed the importance of proper breathing in producing adequate breath support for speaking. Phonation has to do with the actual producing of the sound as the breath passes through the vocal folds. Resonation concerns the amplifying of the sound by the cavities of the mouth, throat, and nose.

Phonation and resonation are complex physiological functions. This book cannot really touch upon all of the factors involved in the two processes. Some preachers may have difficulties in either producing or amplifying sound, but those problems are the concern of the medical specialists. If you have trouble in those areas, I would suggest that you consult a good speech pathologist or throat specialist. For the most part, though, phonation and resonation cannot be consciously improved through the procedures I recommend in this book. For that reason, we move from the first step in the process of speaking to the last one, articulation.

Articulation is the process of forming the sounds that characterize connected speech. The air that vibrates in the mouth and nose is modified by the tongue, the lower jaw, the lips, and the hard and soft palates.[1] Articulation is that process which transfers mere sound into speech sounds. Articulation is synonymous with *enunciation.* It should not be confused with *pro*nunciation.

1. Judson S. Crandell and Gerald M. Phillips, *Speech: A Course in Fundamentals* (Glenview, Ill.: Scott Foresman, 1963), p. 35.

Pronunciation has to do with the correctness of the sounds and accents in spoken words. Articulation, on the other hand, has to do with the shaping of those sounds by the lips, teeth, tongue, and hard and soft palates.[2]

The preacher who wants to communicate the Word of God effectively to his listeners will be concerned about articulation. If he fails to properly articulate his words, the ability of the congregation to understand what he is saying will be greatly diminished. One congregation complained about its preacher: "For six days a week he is invisible, and on the seventh he is inaudible." Take pains to ensure that those who listen to you can understand what you are saying. Learning to articulate properly will greatly improve your sermon delivery.

Articulation is a key ingredient in achieving maximum relaxation during sermon delivery. Actually, proper breathing and proper articulation work together. As we have already seen, adequate breath support prepares the vocal mechanism to function in a relaxed manner. Likewise, articulating words properly will enable you to speak with a minimum of tension in the extrinsic muscles. I have found it helpful in practicing for sermon delivery to imagine I am plucking words off my lips as I might pluck the notes off a guitar string. Voice teachers sometimes refer to this as placing the tone. In the strictest sense, waves of sound cannot be directed or placed. However, psychologically there seems to be some advantage to this approach. To think in terms of the words being plucked from the lips has a tendency to relax the throat muscles. This enables the vocal mechanism to function with a minimum of constriction.

Basic Speech Elements

In relation to articulation there are three basic speech elements: vowels, diphthongs, and consonants. Vowels are sounds formed in the resonating cavities as air flows through the mouth. For our purposes, think primarily in terms of letters *A, E, I, O,*

2. Charlotte I. Lee and Frank Galati, *Oral Interpretation* (Boston: Houghton Mifflin, 1977), p. 118.

U. The vowels give color to the sounds of speech. Diphthongs are sounds produced by a combination of two vowel sounds occurring in the same syllable and blending continuously from one to the other without interruption.[3]

The consonants might be regarded as the bones of speech. Whether we say "Good morning!" to the paper carrier or "Good night" to our wife, we cannot communicate by means of vowel sounds alone. Hardly any sounds are expressed without using consonants as well as vowels. Without consonants there would actually be no speech. The correct articulation of the consonants actually does more to assist in adequate vocal communication than does any other factor.

Consonants are produced in three *zones of articulation*. The first zone is found between the lips, that is, between the lower lip and the upper front teeth. Consonants in this group are: *P, B, W, WH, F, V, M.*

The second zone is found between the front teeth, the tip of the tongue, and the hard palate behind the teeth. This groups includes: *T, D, TH, R, S, SH, ZH, Y, N.*

The third zone is formed by the back of the tongue and the soft palate. Included in this group are these consonants: *K, G, NG.*[4]

At this point stop your reading and say each of the letters in the three consonant groups. As you say them, notice where each sound is produced. That will help you learn to place each consonant in its proper position for good articulation. Notice that the tongue, teeth, lips, and hard and soft palates assume different adjustments in relation to each other as the consonants are produced.

Sometimes consonants are explained in terms of the positions of the articulators as they are produced. Those produced by the action of the lips are called *labials*. The labials are also divided into two groups:

3. John A. Grasham and Glenn G. Gooder, *Improving Your Speech* (New York: Harcourt, Brace and World, 1960), p. 161.
4. Friedrich Brodnitz, *Keep Your Voice Healthy* (Springfield, Ill.: Thomas, 1973), p. 48.

1. Those in which only the lips are used:
   W as in wind
   WH as in which
   M as in meat
   P as in pork
   B as in bee

2. Those in which the lips are used along with the teeth:
   F as in father
   V as in very

Consonants produced by the tongue primarily are called *linguals*. The linguals are divided into four groups:

1. Those the tongue forms with the teeth:
   TH as in thick or that

2. Those formed by the tip of the tongue and the hard palate:
   T as in tip
   D as in do
   N as in no
   L as in lip
   R as in row

3. Those formed by the body of the tongue and the hard palate:
   S as in so
   Z as in zebra
   SH as in show

4. Those formed by the tongue and the soft palate:
   C as in cat
   K as in king
   G as in get
   NG as in sing
   Y as in yes[5]

5. David Blair McClosky, *Your Voice at Its Best* (Plymouth, Mass.: Memorial, 1972), pp. 46-48.

How to Improve Articulation

There are several ways the preacher can improve his articulation. One of these is to develop greater flexibility in the tongue, lips, and jaw. Laziness in any of these areas will greatly hinder proper articulation. Diehl and Stevenson have several helpful suggestions for eliminating stiffness in the articulators. First, purse your lips and move them in all possible directions. Next, draw the lips back and forth and then purse them. Stick your tongue out as far as you can. Touch your lower lip and upper lip with the tongue. Move the tongue from side to side. Then rotate the tongue tip slowly around your lips from left to right. Rotate the tongue tip from right to left. Touch the tongue tip to the center of the upper lip, the lower lip, then each corner of your mouth. Lift the tongue tip to the hard palate, then slowly relax it until it is flat in the mouth.[6]

Perhaps you have noticed that chewing is a function very similar to speaking. The same muscles used for speaking are used in chewing. Maybe you have also noticed that you can speak and chew at the same time. To do so is not considered to be good etiquette. However, I have found chewing and speaking at the same time can be helpful in developing flexibility in my articulators. Try this sometime: Imagine you have your mouth filled with food. Then begin to chew like a savage. As you chew, with exaggerated movements of the mouth, tongue, and teeth, slowly begin to add speech. This exercise will do wonders in correcting stiffness in your articulators. The approach was popular among German speech therapists in correcting vocal disorders. Although the method has not gained wide acceptance in this country, I have found it helps me a great deal in relaxing my lips, mouth, and tongue.

Articulation Drills

Here are several articulation drills to help you practice articulation:

6. Dwight E. Stevenson and Charles F. Diehl, *Reaching People from the Pulpit* (Grand Rapids: Baker, 1958), p. 152.

1. A coward weeps and wails with woe when his wiles are thwarted.

2. Which whelp whined when he heard the whale wheeze?

3. Men and women may swim in the warm summertime before September storms come upon them.

4. The big, bold baboon grabbed the bare branches with his boney brown hands.

5. The pelican's pouch is primarily appropriate for keeping him supplied with supper.

6. Five elephants huffed and puffed as they filed through the Friday traffic followed by a laughing waif.

7. Vivacious voices strove to give more volume to the various verses.

8. A thousand thoughts about birth and death came thronging to the mind of the thin, unhealthy youth.

9. They scythed the withering grass beside the smooth paths.

10. Try to take the time to teach Patty a pleasant tune.

11. Cheerful Cheshire cats chew chunks of chopped chicken and choke down chestnuts and cheese.

12. Day after day the good old educators try to din adequate knowledge into dreamy dunces.

13. An honest scientist needs no hindrance in his sound investigation into the wonders of the universe.

14. Violins and lutes played lovely tunes as the pale silver moonlight filtered through the olive trees.

15. Ripe, round, bright red berries drenched with rich cream provide thorough pleasure to those who truly relish fruit.

16. Susan sighed softly as she passed the nice Swiss physicist in the passageway.

17. At the zoo the lazy visitors observe zebras, gazelles, lizards, and prize lions.

18. She shed her mesh shoes and shamelessly shook her freshly washed shawl from her shoulders.

19. We usually derive composure and pleasure from leisure.

20. The jealous major became enraged at the adjutant's jolly jokes about his huge budget.

21. The kindly king and his quiet queen liked pickled pig's knuckles with their cooked cabbage and crusty kidney pie.

22. The gay ghost ogled the gaping guests, then wagged its gray finger at them as it gathered the garnets together.

23. Bring me a spring song to sing for the waiting throng.

24. The distinguished Englishman learned the Anglo Saxon language and wrote singular jingles in it.

25. The monkey blinked and wrinkled his pink nose as he tinkled the clinking trinkets on his ankles.

26. Last year the yew in the canyon beyond our yard turned yellow.

27. Harry, the hunter, has hiked home through the hills
     since he heard that a huge horse's hoof print was beheld
     in Hiram's Hollow.[7]

Here is another good drill you might like to use to improve
your articulation:

Retreating and beating and meeting and cheating,
delaying and straying and playing and spraying,
advancing and prancing and glancing and dancing,
recalling, turmoiling and toiling and boiling,
and gleaming and streaming and steaming and beaming,
and rushing and flushing and brushing and gushing,
and flapping and wrapping and clapping and slapping,
and curling and whirling and purling and twirling,
and thumping and plumping and dumping and jumping,
and dashing and flashing and splashing and clashing;
and so never ending, but always descending, sounds and
motions forever and ever are blending, all at once and
all o'ver with a mighty uproar; and this way the water
comes down at the Lodore.[8]

Southey, "The Cataract of Lodore"

Spend some time each day going over a few of these articulation drills. As you practice them, overexaggerate the motions
of your articulating organs. Think about what sounds you are
forming. But do not work on articulation during the delivery of a
sermon. You might become so involved in proper articulation
that you overarticulate. That can be as detrimental to your sermon delivery as is poor articulation. Gradually work on this area
of speech production. Do not go to seed over it.

Work on the three areas we have discussed in these opening
chapters. You will be amazed at how much your vocal delivery
will improve. You will not solve all the problems of adequate
vocal production, but you will be working on the key ingredients
in good vocal presentation. The next chapter will help you learn
how to put together a variety of vocal variables to enhance the
effectiveness of your speaking.

7. McClosky, pp. 52-57. Used by permission.
8. William G. Hoffman, *How to Make Better Speeches* (New York: Funk & Wag-
    nalls, 1976), p. 171.

4

Integrating

The vocal aspects of delivery must be correctly integrated if sermon delivery is to be effective. We have laid the two foundational elements in good vocal production—good breathing and proper articulation. At this point, however, most delivery problems that plague preachers become apparent.

This chapter is not intended to be a "quick fix" for all the sermon delivery problems you may experience. Rather, we want to isolate several variables that must be properly coordinated to make it possible for you to preach in an appealing, attractive, and compelling manner.

I have placed these variables into four couplets on the basis of the relation of each one to the other: rate and pace; volume and stress; phrasing and pause; pitch and inflection.

Rate and Pace

Rate has to do with the speed with which we speak. Speech rate may be measured by the number of words spoken divided by the minutes that elapse during the speaking. Each person has his own rate of speaking. Acceptable speaking rates normally vary between 120 and 160 words per minute. There are no hard, fast rules—delivery is considered acceptable when the listeners are able to grasp what the speaker says. Communication is hindered when one speaks too fast or too slow.

The tendency of young preachers is to talk too fast. A sermon should be delivered with excitement and vigor. But in his enthusiasm the young preacher may speak too fast to be understood clearly by his listeners. Rapid delivery does communicate a sense of excitement. But any sound, no matter how exciting it may be at the beginning, will lose attention if it is continued without any variation. Niagara Falls is hardly noticed by those who live nearby.[1]

If you speak too rapidly you will not be understood, and you may leave your listeners out of breath. There are other reasons preachers talk too fast. Many speak rapidly because they are quick thinkers and fluent in speech. I do not recommend that you radically change your rate, if rapidity is natural to you. To do so risks developing an artificial style that communicates something other than what you are. Instead, make an effort to slow down just a bit, and use other devices of speech to keep the rate from becoming difficult to follow. A wonderful help in regulating a rapid delivery is pause, which we will discuss later in the chapter.

A too-rapid rate suggests nervousness and lack of ease. Remember that every second does not have to be filled with sound. To move on at a frantic pace may convey to the listeners a sense of personal insecurity and uncertainty about the message.

Spurgeon has this to say about too rapid speech:

> Excessively rapid speaking, tearing and raving into utter rant, is quite inexcusable; it is not, and never can be powerful, except with idiots, for it turns what should be an army of words into a mob, and most effectually drowns the sense in floods of sound. It is an infliction not to be endured twice, to hear a brother who mistakes perspiration for inspiration, tear along like a wild horse with a hornet in its ear until he has no more wind, and must need to pause to pump his lungs full again; a repetition of this indecency several times in a sermon, is not uncommon, but is most painful. Pause soon enough to prevent that cough, which rather creates pity for the breathless orator than sympathy with the subject in hand.[2]

1. William G. Hoffman, *How to Make Better Speeches* (New York: Funk & Wagnalls, 1976), p. 196.
2. Charles H. Spurgeon, *Lectures to My Students* (London: Marshall, Morgan and Scott, 1954), p. 115.

The other tendency is to speak too slowly. This is the tendency of the older preacher. As one matures the mind has a tendency to slow down. The thoughts normally do not come as rapidly as they once did. Also, the older preacher may not have the physical vigor he once had. All of us have had the experience of listening to some dear brother who spoke so slowly that we found it difficult to stay with him. Our minds were constantly going off on little mental excursions. Avoid speaking so slowly that your listeners have to constantly work at listening to you.

The rate of your delivery becomes your helper when you use it with variety. The rate should never be constant. To speak too fast or too slow all the time is deadly to effective delivery. Be constantly changing your rate. Less important content may be spoken more quickly. The more important statements of your sermon may be slowed down for emphasis.

The size of the building in which you speak will have much to do with your rate. Adjust your rate to suit the size of the building. A smaller room will allow you to speak a bit faster. The larger the room, the greater the reverberation. This means you must be more deliberate as you speak.

The intellectual and emotional content of what you are saying should also guide you in the rate you use. Grief and contempt are slow. Joy and enthusiasm are faster.[3]

Pace is related to rate of speaking. Good delivery has a sense of pace. The sermon marches. There is a sense of movement about the sermon. I have just suggested that your rate should never be constant. This is certainly true. But all through the message there should be a sense of flow. Some refer to this as fluency. Though a change in pace is needed all through the message, there should be an absence of hesitation as the rate is suited to the desired meanings of the words said. The thoughts and emotions conveyed should alter pacing appropriately as you proceed through the message. Your sermon should never sound as if you have memorized it or as if you are reading it. Your sermon should demonstrate the same flexibility in rate and pace as in your everyday speech.

3. Grand Fairbanks, *Voice and Articulation Drillbook* (New York: Harper & Row, 1940), p. 112.

Volume and Stress

Volume is the amount of sound you use to say what you say. Volume is essential to delivery. If the preacher cannot be heard, then nothing else matters. On the other hand, if the preacher speaks with too much volume, he sounds unnatural and oppressive.[4]

Regrettably, preachers have a tendency to go to extremes in the use of volume. The preacher is either so soft he cannot be heard or so loud the ears of the people are overwhelmed.

Spurgeon has a few choice words to say about preachers who use too much volume: "Two or three earnest men now present are tearing themselves to pieces by needless bawling; their poor lungs are irritated and their larynx inflamed by boisterous shouting, from which they seem unable to refrain."[5] Spurgeon continues: "Be a little economical with that enormous volume of sound. In fact, too much noise stuns the ear, creates reverberations and echos, and effectually injures the power of your sermons."[6]

The key in the use of volume is again variety. Volume should be governed by content. A change in volume indicates the importance of what is being said. Volume may be a great help in giving proper emphasis to important ideas you hope to convey to your audience. There are times when you should open all the stops. But if you are loud all the time, then nothing you say will receive appropriate emphasis by means of volume.

There are also times a whisper can be even more effective than a loud exclamation. Why not vary your degrees of loudness? Try going from a whisper to a roar and from a roar to a whisper.[7] Again, allow the content of your sermon to dictate the appropriate use of volume. Do not make the mistake of thinking that mere loudness is evidence of preaching in the power of the Holy Spirit. To be sure, there are times the Holy Spirit will uti-

---

4. Hoffman, p. 99.
5. Spurgeon, p. 116.
6. Ibid.
7. Milton Dickens, *Speech: Dynamic Communication* (New York: Harcourt Brace Jovanovich, 1954), p. 186.

lize the full capacity of your vocal strength. Do not forget, however, that sometimes the Lord speaks in a still, small voice.

Stress may be considered the intensity or the force we use—the emphasis on the words that count in what we are saying.[8] Certain ideas in every sentence are primary. Other ideas take a more subordinate place. Failure to distinguish properly between the important and the unimportant causes our speech to lack emphasis and clear meaning.[9] The use of proper stress can be just as effective as volume in conveying what we want to say. We stress a word by making it stand out in a phrase. We may do this by means of higher pitch, longer duration of tone, or increased volume. Choose the words that are to receive prominence in what you say and focus your attention on them. Give stress to the thought-bearing words in your sentences.[10]

Nouns, verbs, adjectives, and adverbs usually carry most of the meaning and therefore need high intensity. On the other hand, conjunctions, articles, prepositions, and pronouns usually have lower intensity.[11] As you listen to others in normal conversation, notice the words they emphasize. Notice how effective communicators stress certain key words in their phrases and sentences.

Coupling volume and stress will enable you to be much more effective in your sermon delivery. Project your voice according to the size of the room in which you speak. Generally, you will need enough volume to reach every person in the room. Be constantly aware of your audience. By means of your voice reach out to your audience with every sentence. Do not think, however, in terms of throwing your voice at your listeners. Rather, speak as if you were hitting baseballs—hitting high flies to your audience instead of low grounders. Hit them up and over to the people. Give the sense that you know what you are doing. Convey the awareness that volume and stress are your servants.

8. Hoffman, p. 99.
9. Ibid., p. 191.
10. Robert King, *Forms of Public Address* (Indianapolis: Bobbs-Merrill, 1969), p. 80.
11. Fairbanks, p. 122.

Keep in mind again that variety is the key. Vary your volume. Give appropriate stress to the most important words in your sentences and phrases. Deemphasize nonessential words. Further, use volume and stress together to increase the listenability of your sermon. Use stress sometimes instead of volume for emphasis. Give a word a higher pitch with increased volume. Then, speak a word on a lower pitch with less volume. Always subjugate volume and stress to the ideas you seek to convey.

Pitch and Inflection

Pitch has to do with the movement of the voice up and down the scale in different registers with various inflections. This is the melody of your voice.[12] Proper use of pitch is a vital factor in increasing the attractiveness of sermon delivery.

A distinction needs to be made between habitual pitch and optimum pitch. Habitual pitch is the level on the scale at which you most often speak. Optimum pitch is the level at which your voice functions best. They may not be the same.[13] Each human voice has an appropriate pitch. Naturally, this pitch changes during the maturing of the voice, but once puberty has been passed there is a pitch that is best for your voice. You may easily find your optimum pitch. Using a piano, sing down to the lowest note you can comfortably sing. Go up the scale five piano keys. This will usually be the pitch you should use most of the time. Check tapes of your sermons to see if you are speaking for the most part at your optimum level. Young preachers especially have a tendency to develop an habitual pitch different from their optimum one. They want to sound mature and impressive, so they push their voices into the lower registers. This puts an unhealthy strain upon the vocal folds and creates an unnatural sound. Each preacher must be willing to accept the voice God has given him. That voice must then be trained and developed to its fullest extent.

12. Haddon W. Robinson, *Biblical Preaching* (Grand Rapids: Baker, 1980), p. 204.
13. Anna Lloyd Neal, *A Syllabus for Fundamentals of Speech* (Greenville, S.C.: Bob Jones U., 1977), p. 36.

The preacher will be wise to utilize as wide a variety in pitch as possible. A good preacher distributes his voice over a range of approximately two octaves. Do not be content to stay within a restricted range. Fully utilize all the notes the Lord has given you in your vocal instrument.

Spurgeon describes the importance of using the full range of your vocal instrument: "Brethren, in the name of everything that is sacred, ring the whole chime in your steeple, and do not dun your people with the ding-dong of one poor cracked bell."[14] Spurgeon further appeals for variety in vocal pitch: "I have often in this room compared the voice to a drum. If the drummer should always strike in one place on the head of his drum, the skin would soon wear into a hole; but how much longer it would have lasted him if he had varied his thumping and had used the entire surface of the drum-head! So it is with a man's voice. If he uses always the same tone, he will wear a hole in that part of the throat which is most exercised in producing that monotony."[15]

The older preachers used to give this kind of advice about pitch: "Start low, go slow; rise higher, strike fire." This was their way of saying that it is normally good to start in the lower pitch levels. This will enable you to rise in pitch as you warm to the sermon. To start in the very highest pitch leaves you nowhere to go later on in the message. Do not be afraid to drop into the lower range at certain key points in your sermon. Those ranges can be very effective. If you throw force into them, they will be heard as well as your higher notes.

Inflection is a change of pitch within a syllable or word. By means of inflection the preacher may express a question, convey sarcasm, express conviction, or suggest doubt. Good inflections greatly enhance the understandability and the interest of what the preacher says.

The direction of the inflection indicates what you are trying to say. For instance, a rising inflection indicates the mind is looking forward. Rising inflections suggest question, doubt, uncertainty, or incompleteness. Consider these statements: Is this your

14. Spurgeon, p. 111.
15. Ibid., p. 119.

book? Are you going to *town?* When book and town are said with raising inflection, question and uncertainty are conveyed.

Downward inflections are generally used to indicate a thought is being completed. An inflection that falls toward the end gives the impression of certainty, emphasis, and strong affirmation. For example: This is your *pen.* A circumflex inflection indicates irony, innuendo, sarcasm, cynicism, or skepticism. Consider these statements: *Well, look* who's here! *Who* do you think you *are?*[16] A flat inflection indicates disappointment or disgust. Consider this statement: I can't go. It is all over.

Length of inflection is also important in conveying meaning. The most important word in a sentence is usually given the longer inflection. Length of inflection very often will indicate the degree of importance of what is said. Intensity and excitement are also indicated.

Abruptness of inflection is also important. A gradual change in inflection indicates calmness, repose, contemplation, and command. On the other hand, an abrupt inflection indicates excitement, intensity, and vigor.

A story about Mark Twain vividly illustrates the part inflection plays in carrying the meaning of what you say. Mark Twain was known as a profane man. His language was often very shocking. His wife, Olivia, tried desperately to break him of the habit of swearing. Getting ready for dinner on an occasion, he was frantically working with the collar button of his dress shirt. The button slipped through his fingers and rolled under the dresser out of sight. From his lips came some of his most spectacular speech. Olivia was disgusted and angry. She decided to teach him a lesson to shame him. Word for word she repeated what Mark had said, then defiantly waited for his reply. Mark looked at her silently for a time, then said, "Livy, you got the words right, but the tune's all wrong."[17]

Proper inflection of words may best be achieved through clear thinking about what you are going to say. Your sermon should have enough mental pictures to create expressive inflec-

---

16. John Eisenson, *Voice and Diction* (New York: Macmillan, 1974), p. 100.
17. Hoffman, p. 200.

tion in your words. More will be said about this in the section on the mental aspects of sermon delivery.

Phrasing and Pause

Phrasing. We actually speak our sentences in a series of words organized into units of thought. We group our words and sentences by thoughts. These word groups are called phrases. One might say that a phrase is a continuous utterance bound by pauses. Phrases aid us in expressing what we want to say, and they aid the listener in understanding what we say. Phrasing is one of the most important tools of the preacher.

King says that proper phrasing is simple. He says it is just a matter of starting where you should and stopping where you should![18] Most of us who speak frequently do not find phrasing to be that easy. Much thought and effort must be placed into properly arranging the words into good thought units. Some phrases may be spoken quickly, giving little force to them. Other phrases are more significant. They must be spoken with more emphasis and more slowly.

There is a relationship between good phrasing and breathing. The preacher must learn to breathe before and after complete thought units. Breathing must be coordinated with phrases so that the thought unit will not be interrupted as the preacher stops for breath, for if the preacher interrupts the thought unit he is likely to hinder good understanding of what he is trying to say.

Pause. Pauses are the punctuation marks of speech. They are the commas, periods, and exclamation points of our language. King defines pauses as momentary silences in communicating meaning.[19] Rudyard Kipling said, "By your silence you shall speak."[20] Actually, pauses are not merely times of silence. Pauses can be meaningful in the delivery of a sermon. Every good preacher knows the value of a pause placed at just the right

18. King, p. 80.
19. Ibid.
20. In Robinson, p. 206.

point. An effective pause is an excellent way to emphasize the punch line.[21]

Pauses serve a multitude of purposes. They permit variety in the voice. They help the preacher keep his speaking rate from becoming too fast. They enable him to regulate his pace so that his sermon delivery is convincingly like that of conversation. Pauses enable the preacher to keep his pitch level from raising to a nervous squeak. By the use of a pause the preacher may indicate a change of topic. Pauses encourage better stress and inflection on significant words and phrases.[22]

Pause is not to be confused with hesitation. Hesitation is empty silence—the silence of frozen forgetting. Pause is eloquent and meaning=conveying silence.[23]

Pauses help the preacher physically. They allow him opportunity to replenish his supply of breath. They assist him mentally. When he pauses the preacher looks ahead to his next thought. Pauses assist the preacher psychologically as well. During pauses he may look at the listeners. As he does so, he can gauge whether or not the people understand what he is saying. A pause may be used effectively before an important word, calling attention to the word. A pause may heighten the dramatic effect of what the preacher is saying. The preacher must be careful, though, to see that his pauses are not all of the same length. Without adequate, well-timed pauses, his sermon will sound rattled off.

Pauses also serve the people. Whereas for the preacher a pause primarily looks forward, for the people the pause primarily looks backward. A pause gives the people opportunity to think about what the preacher has just said. It gives them opportunity to think, to feel, and to mentally and emotionally respond to the content of his words. The people are given a brief mental digestion time. There is a sense, as well, in which pauses allow the people to look forward. A well-timed pause may create in the

21. Mary Forrest and Margot A. Olson, *Exploring Speech Communication* (St. Paul: West, 1981), p. 97.
22. Hoffman, p. 100.
23. Ibid., p. 196.

congregation a sense of anticipation and interest in what the preacher is going to say next.

Pauses should be used properly. Avoid the tendency to fill the silence with speech tics such as *ur, and, uh*. Robinson calls them "word whiskers."[24] For the preacher, such "filler" words may be *praise the Lord, Amen, glory to God*. There is certainly nothing wrong with saying any of those things, but if you use them capriciously to fill in your pauses, you will rob them of their spiritual meaning and impact. You will instead convey a sense of nervousness. Do not be afraid to use pause. It can do much for your sermon delivery. Do not be afraid of silence. Silence can be one of the most meaningful times of the sermon.

Monotony

A proper use of the vocal variables we have mentioned will go a long way toward solving the problem of monotony in delivery. There is probably nothing as devastating to effective sermon delivery as monotony. People are put to sleep when there is a constant recurrence of any of the vocal variables. Sometimes preachers develop certain speech habits that make them very difficult to listen to. These habits are called ministerial whines or tunes. Normally these whines or tunes involve a combination of pitch, rate, inflection, and volume patterns.

The ministerial whine is sometimes developed by the preacher in an attempt to add authority and importance to what he says. The preacher's voice sounds as if he has a steeple in his throat. Actually, he accomplishes the opposite of his intention. People are repulsed by such monotonous, pious speech. All of us have had the experience of listening to a preacher with an affected sound. The preacher needs to speak as a real man to real men. He must rigorously eliminate from his vocal delivery any inkling or tendency to ministerial whine. The availability of tape recording in our day makes it inexcusable for a preacher to be monotonous in his delivery. A constant monitoring of his sermon deliv-

24. Robinson, p. 206.

ery will assist the preacher in catching any recurring speech patterns that cause his delivery to be dead, uninteresting, or offensive.

Take away variety in volume, pitch, inflection, or phrasing, and what remains in the speech lacks luster and sparkle. Spurgeon says: "A preacher can commit ministerial suicide by harping on one string, when the Lord has given him an instrument of many strings to play upon."[25] Be unpredictable in your delivery. Learn to use combinations in the vocal variables. Vary the rate of your speech, slowing down or speeding up at different parts of your message. Pause frequently. Use good and different inflections for your words. Produce variety in your delivery by various degrees of loudness. Alter your pitch. A combination of all these will contribute greatly to vocal variety. Your delivery will be much easier to listen to. The people will not have to force themselves to listen. They will not be able to keep themselves from listening.

As you have studied this section on the mechanical aspects of delivery you may have experienced a common apprehension. Perhaps you know a preacher who studied speech with the result that his sermon delivery was actually made worse rather than better. All of us are anxious to convey the gospel truth with the fervor and excitement deeply embedded in our souls. We do not want anything to hinder our being able to do that in our preaching.

Vocal training need not produce that result. Rather, attention to the mechanical aspects of delivery can assist the preacher in making his delivery more powerful than ever before. His sermons can still be on fire. As he preaches the thunder can clap; the lightning can crack. The content of this chapter is designed to show how to use the vocal variables properly. It is also to show how to avoid misuse of the vocal variables. When the preacher uses the vocal variables in the way he should, his sermon delivery will be lively and dynamic.

In closing, let me suggest some exercises that will help you improve your integration of the vocal variables. One of the most

---

25. Spurgeon, p. 111.

helpful exercises is to read Scripture aloud. I recommend reading certain selections from the Bible to help you with the various aspects of vocal delivery. The psalms are excellent to develop proper breathing, phrasing, pitch change, and rate. Take a short psalm. Study its content. Determine how to put it into good phrases. Mark where your pauses will be. Determine where you need to change your vocal pitch. Ask yourself where you should speed up or slow down your delivery. The psalms lend themselves quite well to this kind of drill.

The material in 1 Samuel is excellent for developing proper integration of rate, phrasing, and inflection. Read several of the chapters. Again, be sure each of the vocal variables reflects the meaning of what is being said.

The gospel of Luke is a good portion of Scripture to use in improving pitch, inflection, phrasing, and pause. As you read the gospel narrative, take note of its descriptive dialogue. The readings in Luke, like those in 1 Samuel, will help you greatly.

The following selection will help you master phrasing and pause. Also, the words in the selection can give you training in change of pitch and inflection. The selection as a whole can help you learn how to speed up or slow down your rate of speaking.

Death Speaks
W. Somerset Maugham

There was a merchant in Bagdad who sent his servant to market to buy provisions, and in a little while the servant came back, white and trembling, and said, "Master, just now when I was in the marketplace I was jostled by a woman in the crowd and when I turned I saw it was Death that jostled me. She looked at me and made a threatening gesture; now, lend me your horse and I will ride away from the city and avoid my fate. I will go to Samarra and there Death will not find me." The merchant lent him his horse, and the servant mounted it, and he dug his spurs in its flanks and as fast as the horse could gallop he went. Then the merchant went down to the marketplace and he saw me standing in the crowd and he came to me and said, "Why did you make a threatening gesture to my servant when you saw him this morning?" "That was not a threatening gesture," I said, "it was only a start of surprise. I was astonished to see him in Bagdad, for I had an appointment with him tonight in Samarra!"[26]

26. From the play *Sheppey* (New York: Doubleday, Doran, 1934).

5

Improving the Voice

You are obviously interested in improving your sermon delivery or you would not be reading this book. The subjects considered thus far have given the basic information needed to point you toward improvement in sermon delivery. Actually, every man called to the ministry should avail himself of every opportunity for special training in the areas of voice and speech. I believe all ministerial students should be required to take several courses in voice as part of their preparation for the ministry. If that is not possible, he should make an effort on his own to train the voice God has given him.

In this chapter I want to make several suggestions about how to improve your voice. Obviously, some preachers are blessed with voices of finer quality than others. Nothing can be done about the size or texture of the vocal folds. Wise is the preacher who does not try to speak in a deeper voice than his optimum pitch allows. Wiser is the preacher who uses the voice God has given him to the fullest level of efficiency. But even if you never become a master of sermon delivery, with hard work you can considerably improve your delivery over a period of years.

The first step is to study carefully the basic processes involved in voice production. Reread the first four chapters and use them as a starting point for increasing your understanding of the principles of voice production. Learn all you can about your voice. This can only help you be a better communicator.

A study of the vocal mechanism will help you discover any vocal problems you may have. In making this discovery you will be able to improve those problems on your own or will realize the need to consult an expert. In most cities there are good throat specialists and speech pathologists.

Voice Evaluation

A personal study of your own voice can be productive. A study of this type is easier for preachers today than it has ever been before. My own sermons have been taped for many years. I spend a great deal of time while driving evaluating my own sermon delivery. But let me warn you—be prepared for a surprise when you first hear yourself speak! You probably will not sound on tape as you sound to yourself while you are preaching. When you listen to yourself on a tape you are hearing how you sound to the ears of others. When you are actually preaching you are hearing the sound of your voice through the bones and nerves of your mouth and head. There is a difference. Don't let yourself become discouraged. You are probably not as bad as you may sound to yourself. You may not be as *good* as you sound to yourself either!

Listen to every sermon you preach. As you listen to your sermon, pay attention to the various aspects of delivery. Ask yourself, How could I have said that better? Stop the tape and rephrase it aloud. Some preachers find it helpful to have a little chart listing all the vocal variables mentioned in chapter 4. Listen to your sermon, keeping those in mind. Rate yourself on each of them.

For instance, is your volume too loud or too low? Does your delivery demonstrate good variety in volume? What about your rate? Are you speaking too fast or too slowly? Do you vary your rate enough to avoid monotony? Do you stay in the same pitch too long? Is your inflection consistent with what you are saying? What about your phrasing? Are your words grouped together well? Do you utilize pause in order to breathe correctly and to help prepare yourself for what you want to say next? The purpose is not to evaluate the content of your sermon. Rather, you are concerned about how the content was delivered. Constantly ask yourself: How could I have said this better?

You will be surprised how much this analysis can help to improve your delivery. If you do not listen to yourself constantly, you will tend to lapse into poor vocal habits. I want to emphasize in the strongest terms possible the necessity of doing a week-by-week evaluation of your sermon delivery. The time spent in the effort will richly repay you in the improvement of your preaching.

Study Effective Preachers

Another step in improving your voice is to study the delivery of good preachers. Select several preachers you consider to be superior in sermon delivery. Study the delivery of men who are effective communicators. See what they do. Listen to them, not for what they say, but for how they say what they say. Learn from them. Do not imitate their styles, but glean from them helpful ideas about how to improve your own delivery.

There are also men in secular fields who can help you improve your delivery. Many of today's television commentators are well trained in the use of their voices. Notice how they speak. Learn from them.

Warren Wiersbe has said, "There is both a science and an art to preaching, and you need to learn both." He continues: "The art of preaching is something you learn from a successful preacher, a role model."[1] Wiersbe further adds: "In one sense preaching is not taught—it is caught. Happy is that student who somewhere meets a teacher or preacher who lights a fire in his soul."[2]

Self-improvemnt

My fourth suggestion for improving your voice is to establish a regular program of self-improvement. Several books on voice give a plan of vocal improvement to be followed, but I suggest that you develop your own. There are some ingredients

1. Warren W. Wiersbe and David Wiersbe, *Making Sense of the Ministry* (Chicago: Moody, 1983), p. 109.
2. Ibid., p. 112.

in any program of sermon delivery that should be followed. I suggest that you study the vocal aspects of delivery one by one. Spend some time on the matters of volume and stress. Work for a while on rate and pace. Then spend some time working on phrasing and pause. Later, study the use of pitch and inflection. Work on proper breathing and correct articulation. Try to isolate any problems you may have in these areas. Locate whatever problems may be apparent. Work on one aspect of vocal delivery at a time.

A good way to improve your sermon delivery is to read aloud. By reading aloud you can check yourself on how well you are using the various mechanical aspects of speech. In addition, you can check to see if you are breathing properly, and you can work on your rate of delivery. Do not read only prose. Reading good poetry is sometimes an excellent drill for practice in vocal delivery.

In the previous chapter I indicated certain sections of Scripture that can be helpful as you work on improving sermon delivery. There is also profit to be derived from reading printed sermons. I have found the sermons of Charles Spurgeon to be especially helpful. Try reading some of Spurgeon's sermons aloud. As you read them, practice all the aspects of delivery.

Practice!

Whatever plan you have, you must put that plan into action. Plan your program. Practice your plan. There is need for caution at this point: All your efforts for improving vocal delivery should be done *outside* the pulpit. A mistake I made as I learned more about the vocal mechanism and how to use it properly was to try consciously to implement those improvements in my sermons on Sunday. The results were disastrous. I found myself involved in real mental gymnastics. The preacher who preaches without notes has enough mental activity as it is. To carry to the pulpit the added load of thinking about all the aspects of sermon delivery is more than the normal mind can bear. Jay Adams expresses my thought concerning this quite well: "Such thoughts [about vocal delivery] must not be allowed to come to mind during the delivery of the sermon itself. It is self-defeating for a preacher to think about the delivery he is using when preaching. Where proper practice takes place you will soon find new habits begin to bleed over into one's speech."[3]

Do your practicing outside the pulpit. Through your reading out loud and the use of the exercises in the previous chapters, you will correct poor habits and develop proper habits of speech. Then, put these new habits to work in your daily conversations. Through much practice the improvements will carry over into your pulpit delivery.

Sometimes a sympathetic friend can assist you. This should be someone who is genuinely interested in helping you improve your delivery. Your wife may be willing to do this. If she is able to work with you in this manner, she may be a great help. But do avoid trouble at the pastorium! If she can help you without difficulty, do not hesitate to let her. Whomever you use, the point is that you need someone other than yourself to point out flaws that you do not notice in your sermon delivery.

Practice until improvement comes. Do not expect to have a brand new speaking voice overnight. Many very gifted singers remain students of voice all their lifetimes. The preacher should look upon improving his sermon delivery as a lifelong enterprise. Vocal improvements do not come easily. Neither do you correct faulty speech patterns in a few sessions. Work on improving your delivery weekly. Practice until good vocal habits become second nature to you. Do not become obsessed with sermon delivery, however. It is only one aspect of your preaching assignment, albeit an important one. To focus unduly on your sermon delivery can actually create problems for you during the delivery of your sermons. Bacon says: "The quality of the vocal instrument is important because flexibility of the instrument increases the range of things it can encompass. Nevertheless, experience has shown that too narrow a focus on such matters often produces an interpretor more concerned with his instrument than with his

---

3. Jay Adams, *Pulpit Speech* (Phillipsburg, N.J.: Presbyterian and Reformed, 1971), p. 40.

music."[4] The preacher can get so interested in his voice that he fails to adequately convey his message. Your voice is a tool, not an altar.

You only have one voice. God has given it to you. Use that one voice to the fullest extent of its capabilities. Do not be satisfied to allow your voice to be less than it can be by proper training and practice. Make your vocal instrument a help in communicating the Word of God, not a hindrance.

4. Wallace A. Bacon, *The Art of Interpretation* (New York: Holt, Rinehart, and Winston, 1972), pp. 5-6.

6

Caring for the Voice

Delivering a sermon is rigorous physical activity. Some have estimated that one hour of speaking is the same as six hours of manual labor. Virtually the whole body is involved in delivering a sermon. Stevenson and Diehl have said that to speak loudly the single letter *b* one uses at least 95 different muscles.[1] The weariness the preacher feels after a long day of speaking on Sunday testifies to the tremendous physical exertion involved.

Today's pastor carries a speaking load much heavier than his predecessors. The pastor of a busy, growing congregation in the twentieth century has many speaking demands placed upon him. There are the normal preaching services of the week. Many pastors preach two times, some as many as three times, on Sunday morning. There is also a message to deliver on Sunday night. Increasingly, churches are having full-fledged preaching services on Wednesday night as well. Luncheons, special group meetings, teaching activities, and so on, fill the average pastor's week with a number of speaking responsibilities. In addition to this, pastors very often carry a busy outside speaking schedule. The local civic club calls upon the pastor to speak. Weekly radio messages must be prepared. Preaching in revival meetings in other churches is often part of the pastor's preaching activities. All of these make it important for the preacher to know how to adequately care for his voice.

---

1 Dwight E. Stevenson and Charles F. Diehl, *Reaching People from the Pulpit* (Grand Rapids: Baker, 1958), p. 5.

Vocal Disorders

The preacher may suffer from a variety of vocal disorders. A sore throat many times is the constant companion of the preacher. Strain of the voice, allergies, and changes in the temperature all militate against the preacher's throat. In addition, the preacher may suffer hoarseness and chronic problems with his throat because of failure to use his voice properly. Many preachers can barely speak above a whisper on Monday morning. This is too common to be amusing.

Some vocal disorders are even more serious in nature. The preacher may suffer from chronic laryngitis. There may be varying degrees of hoarseness, huskiness, and throat fatigue on a weekly basis. These disorders can greatly hinder the preacher in fulfilling his various speaking assignments. Bowed vocal folds can also become a problem. Instead of remaining straight, the edges of the folds curve because of incorrect muscular function.

An even more serious problem the preacher may develop is the vocal nodule. Normally vocal nodules are caused by incorrect use of the voice, although sometimes they are caused by allergies. A nodule on a vocal fold almost invariably appears on the anterior third. A nodule is much like a corn on the toe. It is a danger signal of the greatest importance.

Vocal nodules are detected in a variety of ways. The preacher's voice begins to sound breathy. He experiences uncertainty in pitch. Sometimes there is a sudden wavering in his voice. His voice becomes hoarse at the very beginning of a sermon. This hoarseness may even appear in normal conversation. Sometimes the nodule will disappear with a few days of voice rest. In more severe cases some have recommended surgery. Actually, according to the experts in the field, surgery is not the best answer. The original cause of the nodules must be remedied. Nodules may be removed by surgery, but new ones will appear as soon as speaking is resumed if the same speech patterns prevail. The only adequate way to deal with vocal nodules is a radical correction of all mistakes in the use of the voice.[2] If you have a

---

2. Friedrich Brodnitz, *Keep Your Voice Healthy* (Springfield, Ill.: Thomas, 1973), p. 158.

vocal nodule, I urge you to consult a throat specialist who works in cooperation with a qualified voice therapist.

Causes of Vocal Problems

When voice problems appear, they are usually caused by one or more of three bad speaking habits. Some vocal disturbances are due to wrong force. Too much muscular force or force in the wrong places of vocal production may create the problems we have mentioned. Preaching with too much volume over a sustained period of time may cause serious vocal problems.

Second, some voice disturbances come about because of wrong pitch. During the stress and excitement of sermon delivery the muscles near the vocal folds may tense unduly. The voice becomes constricted, throaty, and harsh. This causes the pitch to go up. Under the influence of such prolonged nervous tension this constriction focuses on the vocal folds. It causes the folds themselves to be extremely tight and to bang together at the anterior third in an abusive manner. The third reason for vocal disturbances is wrong breathing. When the breath is not used as an adequate support for speaking, smooth coordination of the vocal mechanism is impossible. Failure to breathe correctly, and thereby maintain a sufficient supply of air during speaking, places too much tension on the muscles of the throat and voice box. The aim of adequate abdominal breathing is to expend a minimum of air for a maximum of vocal effort. When this kind of abdominal breathing does not occur, voice problems may result.

When there is inappropriate force, wrong pitch, and incorrect breathing, vocal disturbances inevitably result. Should you have any of the vocal disturbances I have mentioned, or others, see a qualified throat specialist immediately. The voice of the preacher is essential to his ministry. Do not allow any vocal problems to go unchecked.

Vocal Hygiene

The preacher should have a good program of vocal hygiene. Several conditions influence the voice, such as weather and climate. On humid, muggy days the air we inhale is warm. There is enough moisture in such air to keep our vocal mechanism in good condition. Surprisingly, the nice cool winter days are most dangerous for the voice. Those are the times when we must be especially careful with our voices.

The modern preacher is often involved in traveling from place to place on preaching assignments. In a day's time a preacher may move from one climate to an entirely different one. That can play havoc with the voice. The body must make tremendous adjustments to the changes in weather and climate. If possible, therefore, when you are traveling allow for a day of rest before you are to speak. That will give your vocal mechanism time to adjust to the new atmosphere.

Give some attention to the kind of clothing you wear. Some feel that dressing heavily helps avoid catching colds. Actually, the opposite frequently occurs. Wear sufficient clothing to keep warm but not so much that you begin to perspire.

The home is an important factor in your vocal hygiene. Ensure that your home is properly heated. Also, be careful to have proper ventilation. A stuffy, overheated home can cause problems with your voice.

The preacher should develop good habits of nutrition. Organize your eating around a diet of fresh vegetables, salads, whole grain bread, fruit, and dairy products. Avoid drinking milk before you are to preach. Milk has a tendency to accumulate mucus in the throat. Sweets also create mucus in the throat. The mucus membranes do better with food in which starches are at a minimum.

Be careful about the time you eat your meals. Do not eat a heavy meal before you preach. Perhaps you have experienced eating a heavy meal before preaching. I have ruined some good sermons simply because I was so full I could not speak properly. Also, watch eating excessively *after* you preach. Normally, just after preaching a sermon is a time when tensions are released. You will normally experience greater hunger and thirst at that time than at any other. If you are not careful, this will lead to overindulgence. Eating at late hours, in large portions, can cause poor sleep and overweight.

Plenty of rest is important to good vocal hygiene. Go to bed early the night before you are to preach. I have followed the practice of staying in on Saturday night for many years. That enables me to go to bed early and be fresh the next morning when I am to preach. Also, if at all possible, take your day off on Saturday. A day of relaxation and rest before your main preaching day is highly desirable.

A good exercise program can be helpful to your voice. Good muscle tone will be beneficial to the entire process of speaking. A body in good shape will assist you in preaching in a healthier manner.

Numerous remedies have been suggested for sore and tired throats. Many doctors question the healing value of throat lozenges. Those that contain eucalyptus may even be a hindrance. The cool effect of the eucalyptus may create the impression the throat is better than it is. All we can say positively about throat lozenges is that they stimulate the flow of saliva by movements of the tongue, whatever value this may give you.

The best remedy I have found to help a sore, tired throat is to inhale steam in the shower. Get the water as hot as you can bear it. Fill the bathroom with steam. With mouth wide open, breathe in the steam through your mouth and nose. This will have a soothing, healing effect on your throat.

I have found only one truly effective method of treating colds. Rest. Rest your body so that it has time to fight the infection attacking your vocal organs. If your throat problem persists, consult a throat specialist.

Do your best to avoid speaking when you are experiencing problems with your voice. Sometimes the preacher almost has no choice in the matter. When you must preach even though you experience vocal problems, go as easy as you can.

Avoid using your voice excessively before and after you preach. Conserve your vocal strength. Do not feel you have to sing above all the congregation during the song service. Use the song service to warm your vocal mechanism, not to wear it out. After the service, you may do great damage to your voice by talking loudly and laughing lustily. Your voice is already tired. To talk excessively after preaching merely places undue strain upon your voice. Keep your tones as subdued as possible. Get a good night's sleep. Rest your voice.

Regular Speaking Preferred

The voice will be healthier if you use it as often as possible. That may seem a rather strange statement, but personal experience has proved it to be true. I have many friends who are full-time evangelists. Many of them speak night after night, week after week. Almost all rarely experience voice problems except on those occasions when they go without speaking for a few days. Keep in mind your vocal folds are muscles. Using them frequently will strengthen them. Spurgeon maintained the importance of frequent speaking. "If ministers would speak oftener, their throats and lungs would be less liable to disease. Of this I am quite sure; it is a matter of personal experience and wide observation, and I am confident that I am not mistaken. Gentlemen, twice a week preaching is very dangerous, but I have found five or six times healthy, and even twelve or fourteen not excessive."[3] Spurgeon urged regular daily practice of the voice. "Nothing has a tendency to tire the voice like the occasional prolonged speaking, alternating with long intervals of rest."[4]

Several other factors are important in the care of your voice. The building in which you preach can be a problem for your voice. Some men have actually caused great damage to their voices because they were speaking in poorly designed buildings. Too many buildings are designed for architectural beauty rather than for sight and sound. Poor acoustics can be devastating to the preacher's voice. By all means seek to have adequate sound reinforcement in your church building.

This brings another crucial matter before us in the matter of vocal hygiene. The sound system can help or hurt the voice. Make every effort to have an adequate sound system for your church. There is no excuse for churches today to shackle their

3. Charles H. Spurgeon, *Lectures to My Students* (London: Marshall, Morgan and Scott, 1954), p. 121.
4. Ibid.

preachers with poor sound reinforcement. A good microphone can be a tremendous help in keeping the voice from being abused.

The sound engineer is very important. He can make or break the preacher. He can emphasize the lower or higher frequencies of the preacher's voice. He can completely change the way the preacher sounds. If a sound system is good, the preacher is given support during his speaking. If it is poor, the preacher finds himself battling the microphone. Do your very best to have an adequate sound system in the place where you preach.

Your voice is a delicate, highly complex instrument. Used properly, lives can be touched and blessed. If your voice is not in good condition, you cannot use it to maximum benefit. Take every step necessary to ensure good vocal hygiene.

PART 2

Mental Aspects of Sermon Delivery

One often hears the advice, Learn to use your voice correctly and you will be a good preacher. That advice is fine as far as it goes. The problem is, it does not go far enough. Mastery of the mechanical aspects of delivery will not in itself make you a good preacher. Good vocal technique is certainly important, but it is not the ultimate solution to effective delivery.

Too much attention to the techniques of vocal expression can actually become a subconscious hindrance to the preacher in the act of preaching. The solution is found instead in understanding the processes that produce our flow of words. This takes us behind the spoken words to the mental dynamics that produce them.

In this section I discuss two areas involved in the mental aspects of delivery. The first is mental visualization. The chapter on this subject discusses how the speech process occurs and suggests ways of strengthening your mental images. The basic thrust of the chapter is that delivery is more effective when the preacher learns to see what he says. The next chapter in this section is on mental vitalization. The emphasis of the chapter is on the important task of resurrecting the sermon between the study and the pulpit.

This section will help you understand that you do not have to concentrate merely on the mechanical aspects of delivery. Good mental perception will free you to speak naturally and effectively. The average congregation is much more intelligent than those in previous years. People are much more demanding of their preachers than before. Visual media makes clear to our people the ideas being presented. The preacher must present his ideas with as much clarity as possible. He must not only think in pictures himself, he must enable his people to visualize what he is saying as well.

7

Mental Visualization

When some preachers preach, the people listen with rapt attention. There is an enthusiastic response to what the preacher is saying. The preacher's words are alive and vibrant. On the other hand, some preachers receive little response from the people. People are moving around. The preacher talks on and on, but his words fall upon disinterested ears. Some preachers seem to be able to convey their sermon in an understandable and interesting fashion. Others seem to have little or no ability to generate a favorable response from the people. What is the difference?

Dull Preaching

Jay Adams raises the same question: "Why do you think it is that the average modern congregation is so unaffected and undemonstrative? Could it be—at least in part—because contemporary preachers by dull, lifeless, abstract preaching fail to appeal to their senses?"[1] To be sure, some dullness in the preaching experience can be attributed to a basic lack of interest on the part of people. We are living in times where many seem to have little or no interest in what preachers are saying. But for the most part, people hunger to know what God says in the Bible. If there are inattention and lack of interest, the problem probably originates in the pulpit.

Kirkpatrick shares an imaginary scene: "In colonial times in

1. Jay Adams, *Sense Appeal in the Sermons of Charles Haddon Spurgeon* (Grand Rapids: Baker, 1975), p. 32.

America, an official was appointed in each church, whose duty it was to maintain a keen lookout during the preaching for any member of the congregation who may have fallen asleep. When he discovered such a person, it was his further duty to take in his hand the long stick, one end of which was sharpened to a very fine point. With it he was to walk quietly down the aisle—and prod the preacher!"[2] The primary problem is in the delivery of the preacher. Many have observed a difference between actors and preachers at this point. Actors speak of fiction as if it were real; too many preachers speak truth as if it were fiction.

Preachers do not want to be dull and uninteresting in their delivery. The average pastor is a deeply committed man who seriously desires to communicate God's Word in an effective, interesting, and powerful manner. Why does this desire not communicate itself in the preacher's delivery of his sermon? The difficulty is to be found in a failure to understand the dynamics of mental visualization. Understanding the mental processes of good speaking can do much to cure the preacher of dull, lifeless preaching. Stevenson and Diehl touch on this when they say: "To be alive, a sermon must rise out of the real world of objects, events and persons; and it must throb with this world of color and sound. A living sermon goes back to the grass roots of human experience."[3]

The Mental Processes of Speech

Behind the words we speak are mental images. If these images are alive mentally, then what we say will also be alive. Our speech will be in living color. Several factors are involved in the mental processes of speech. We perceive the world around us by means of sensory images that are important to the speech process, though the exact degree of importance is debated. Some psychologists insist that thinking is entirely imageless. They point out that there are scientists and abstract thinkers who experience

2. Robert White Kirkpatrick, *The Creative Delivery of Sermons* (Joplin, Mo.: Joplin College, 1944), p. 1.
3. Dwight E. Stevenson and Charles F. Diehl, *Reaching People from the Pulpit* (Grand Rapids: Baker, 1958), p. 66.

little or no imagery in their thought processes. For most of us, however, sensory images precede the words we use.

The chain of speech involves four main elements: perception, sensory images, imagination, and words. Let me give a brief definition of each of these. *Perception* is the process of taking stimuli from the world around us and attaching meaning to them. *Sensory images* are those messages sent to the brain by means of our perception. *Imagination* is the mental activity that takes these images and handles them creatively. *Words* are the symbols we use for the objects we perceive. They enable us to place the images we have organized in our minds into forms that can be shared with others. By means of words we are thus able to create in the minds of listeners the same images that are in our minds.

Perception

We perceive the world around us through five primary senses. The visual, our ability to see, is one way we sense the tangible world around us. We are able to see the sky and the clouds. We see the ground and the water. We see the trees and the flowers. Visual stimuli bring all the objects of sight to the brain.

Second, we perceive by means of our auditory sense. This is our ability to hear the countless variety of sounds in our world. We hear the voices of others. We hear the noise of machinery. We hear laughter and singing, crying and shouting.

We also perceive the world around us by means of olfactory sense. All the fragrances and odors of our environment come to our brain through the sense of smell. We smell the sweet roll being cooked in the kitchen. We smell the smoke from the fire. We smell the fragrant perfume worn by our wives.

The world around us is also perceived through our gustatory sense, the sense of taste. We taste the sweetness of honey or the bitterness of a crabapple. We taste the flavor of salt and the yeast of bread.

Fifth, we perceive our environment through our tactile sense. We touch the baby's skin and sense its softness. We sense the coarseness of tree bark by a touch.

Sensory Images

All of these senses constantly bombard our minds with innumerable stimuli. The continuity with which these images flow and correspond to each other in our inner thought processes is what earlier psychologists called the stream of consciousness.[4]

For purposes of speech these sensory perceptions form two kinds of images. First, there are memory images. These images recall the previous sensory experiences, which closely resemble the original perception. The pleasant sights and sounds of an outing at a beautiful country setting with a cool stream, fresh green trees, and melodious birds singing creates certain impressions upon the images of our memory. To recall these images of sound, color, taste, and touch creates vividness and interest in the words we use. They enable us to recreate in our words the reality of those things we have seen and experienced. Second, these perceptions are formed into creative images. Much as the ballet dancer gives creative interpretation of a text through new and imaginative movement, a speaker may take memory images and reconstruct them. Instead of saying, "The stream was a swift one," the speaker may say, "The gurgling stream rushed happily on like a schoolboy bounding from the schoolhouse." These are new units of mental experience. They build upon past original perceptions, but combine and rearrange them into original and unique creations.

Imagination

The ability of the brain to take the original perceptions we have had and arrange them into creative mental images is the work of imagination. The brain spontaneously and sometimes unconsciously rearranges the original perceptions we have had into creative images.

The role of imagination has long been understood as important in the ability of the preacher to present his sermon in an

---

4. Horace G. Rahskoph, *Basic Speech Improvement* (New York: Harper & Row, 1965), p. 108.

effective manner. Whitsell says: "Imagination is one of the most
God-like capacities of man. It plays a significant role in all creative pursuits. The poet, the novelist, the dramatist, the musician,
the painter, the sculptor, and architect would be sadly handicapped without the use of imagination."[5] The same can be said
about the preacher. Every good preacher must know how to use
his powers of imagination effectively. By imagination the preacher
helps the people to see what he is saying. Imagination is a marvelous and distinct gift of God to man. By means of imagination we
are able to conceive of the invisible and make it visible to those
who listen to us preach. Broadus says about imagination: "Without imagination the principles of preaching cannot be utilized in
effective practice. It is regarded by many as the most important
of all factors which go to make the preacher. Imagination is the
imaging function of the mind. It is thinking by seeing, as con-
trasted with reasoning."[6]

To speak in terms of light, sounds, odors, and tastes adds
charm and subtle force to our delivery. If by means of words we
can recreate experiences we have had that are common to our
listeners, our words will be understandable and interesting. The
imagination will enable us to speak in this manner. Imagination
is the difference between a good and an average preacher.

Of course, there is the danger that imagination can run away
with you. But the greater danger is that we will smother our
imagination. The preacher may so analyze Scripture and so dwell
on its contents that he stifles the lively imagery it creates in his
mind. The preacher must use a sanctified imagination if he is to
preach the Scriptures in such a way its truths can be understood
properly. Imagination can transform your sermon from being a
dull lecture into satisfying spiritual food. Warren Wiersbe says:
"A wise use of the principle of hermeneutics will give you information, but you need to add imagination if your ministry is to be
effective. It has well been said that the purpose of a sermon is

---

5. Farris D. Whitsell, *Power in Expository Preaching* (Old Tappan, N.J.: Revell, 1963), p. 103.
6. John A. Broadus, *The Preparation and Delivery of Sermons* (New York: Harper, 1926), p. 279.

not to discuss a subject, but to achieve an object; and that requires a certain amount of imagination."[7]

Improving Imagination

If imagination is so important in the mental aspect of sermon delivery, then we must do everything possible to improve it. Many preachers are gifted with an exceptional imagination. Great preachers have normally been men with this wonderful gift. All preachers, however, may develop their powers of imagination by hard work.

First, you need to understand the process of creativity. Four phases are involved in creativity. The first is preparation. During preparation you need to expose yourself to the widest possible range of information about your subject. As you study a particular passage of Scripture, you will recall all past experience that can be brought to bear upon the passage. By observation you will note every possible detail about the passage. Recall everything you have been able to find about the passage through reading, discussion, and other methods. Study your Scripture passages in such a way that your imagination is involved.

Feel, see, and hear what is going on in the passage. Allow the words actually used to stir your emotional interest. You must read the Scripture passage imaginatively. The entire process of investigating a passage of Scripture can provide necessary material to the imagination. A knowledge of Bible customs, the history of the times, or the circumstances of the writer will provide the raw material with which your imagination can do creative work. You will never be able to recreate with your voice the circumstances of the Scripture unless you learn to read it imaginatively.

Next, there is the time of incubation, when your thoughts are allowed to germinate and mature. This may be a time of rest so that you can digest and assimilate the information you have gathered. Very often a change of activity can be an incubation

7. Warren W. Wiersbe and David Wiersbe, *Making Sense of the Ministry* (Chicago: Moody, 1983), p. 104.

time. Physical exercise, sleep, or rest can be helpful. During this time the subconscious mind is allowed to work on reorganizing the material you have perceived. Put another way, the period spent away from the material will allow your imagination time to rearrange the material into refreshingly new mental images.

Next comes the stage of illumination. This is the moment of insight. New ideas are formed as your imagination has time to work upon them. There are three levels of the work of imagination. Sometimes imagination works in a descriptive manner. As the imagination is fed the facts, the ideas are put into pictures. This enables you to see what may have happened far away and long ago.

Sometimes imagination works in a constructive manner. Facts are synthesized. Things are put together. And sometimes imagination works on the highest level, the creative. This is the time when that which seems to have been dead comes to life. When that happens, it enables the preacher to soar in his thinking.[8]

The fourth stage in the creative process is verification. The new ideas provided you by the work of the imagination are now developed and elaborated. You are ready to take what your imagination has done and place the results into a presentation that can be vivid and picturelike to your listeners.

Another way to strengthen the imagination is to improve your habits of observation. Charles Spurgeon was noted for his ability to speak in pictures. His sermons literally abound in sensory imagery. E. L. Magoon said of Spurgeon: "He has rare powers of observation, recollection, assimilation and creation . . . He seems to have opened his eyes to nature in all its varieties; to science in all its discoveries, and to literature in all its departments."[9] Today's preacher can enhance his delivery considerably by improving his own powers of observation.

That can be done in a variety of ways. You can improve the range of your powers of observation by increasing the breadth of

8. A. W. Blackwood, *Expository Preaching for Today* (Grand Rapids: Baker, 1943), p. 197.
9. E. L. Magoon, *The Modern Whitefield* (New York: Sheldon, Blakeman, 1856), p. 11.

what you have seen and observed. Take opportunities to visit art galleries and museums. Read literature that abounds in imagery. Poetry is especially good in this regard.

You can improve the acuteness of your powers of observation by making the effort to truly look at things, not just glance over them. Take an object and look at it carefully. Notice every possible detail about the object. What kind of materials were used in making it? What is its shape? How big or small is it? What is its color? Its texture? Look at the object from every conceivable perspective.

Your powers of observation through hearing can be improved in the same manner. Stand on a busy street corner. Listen to all the different sounds. Listen to talking voices as people crisscross around you. Listen to the sounds coming from stores nearby. Exhaust every sound that comes to your ears.

Pick up an object. Hold it in your hand. Feel the object. What is it made of? How does it feel? Is it smooth or rough? Touch the object in every possible way.

Such procedures can strengthen your powers of observation. They are not something to be done only for a day or two. Rather, to achieve maximum results, you should make such habits of observation a way of life.

See What You Say

As you strengthen your perception of the stimuli your senses provide the brain, you will be able to think in pictures and thus speak in pictures as well.

See what you say. Relive the mental images that flow behind your words as you speak. Respond so strongly to those images that your words will help your listeners to respond to them as well.

To see what you say and say what you see creates a tremendous sense appeal in your words. Jay Adams explains quite well a mathematical formula for the law of sense appeal. He says: "Sense perception plus synthetic imagination plus realistic description equals sense appeal."[10] By perception we get the

10. Jay Adams, *Pulpit Speech* (Phillipsburg, N.J.: Presbyterian and Reformed, 1971), p. 44.

materials of our mental images. By imagination we organize and arrange them. By description we use words that convey pictures to the minds of our listeners. The result is sense appeal. In a later section on the rhetorical aspects of sermon delivery we will discuss how to use words that increase sense appeal.

Jonathan Edwards had tremendous powers of mental visualization. He was able to paint pictures in his sermons which became very real to his listeners. In his famous sermon, "Sinners in the Hands of an Angry God," he compared the unsaved with a spider or loathsome insect suspended over the flames. He said, "You hang by a slender thread, with the flames of divine wrath flashing about it, and ready every moment to singe and burn it asunder; and you have nothing to lay hold of to save yourself, nothing to keep off the flames of wrath, nothing of your own, nothing that you have ever done, nothing that you can do, to induce God to spare you one moment." So vivid were his words, and so filled with sense appeal, people grasped the pillars and pews of the church to keep from sliding into hell.

George Whitefield could also paint pictures with his words. On an occasion he compared the lost sinner to a helpless blind beggar wandering on the edge of a precipice. He described the poor blind man stumbling forward, his staff slipping from his hands and falling into the abyss. Unconscious of his danger, the beggar stooped down to recover it. Carried away by Whitefield's picture painting ability, a man in the congregation exclaimed, "He's gone! He's gone!"

Be sure that behind the words you speak there is an unending stream of mental images that are made vivid and alive by means of the imagination. This will make your sermon delivery much more powerful and interesting.

When we understand and utilize the mental process of visualization, our delivery is helped in another practical way. To accurately reflect in our words what we see in our minds will enable us to use the mechanical aspects of delivery in a much less mechanical way. As the mind sees clearly each successive idea of the sermon, the voice will tend to naturally express itself in such a way that the ideas will be conveyed correctly. Once the preacher has learned to use his vocal mechanism correctly, its various aspects become the willing servants of the mental images that call forth speech. The preacher will not have to think consciously about matters of volume and rate. He will not have to mechanically phrase his words or use pause at certain times. He will not have to think about how he is going to inflect the words he says. All this will be dictated by the constant stream of sensory images in his mind. The result is a most natural and effective delivery. Visualize what you say, and it will vitalize the words as you speak them.

8

Mental Vitalization

The delivery of a sermon is made effective and compelling when the preacher understands the concept of mental visualization. You can make your sermon come alive by visualizing the mental images and experiencing the emotions of your message while you are saying the words. The words you use and the manner by which you use them will cause your listeners to have strong mental images in their minds. This will enable them to become actively involved in the truths you are conveying in your sermon.

The Sermon Dies

There is an experience common to all preachers. During the preparation of a sermon the preacher discovers truths in God's Word that are tremendously profound and significant. These truths burn in his heart. The message is so on fire that it threatens to burn the paper upon which it is recorded.

The preacher anticipates that the sermon will literally set the people on fire. He can hardly wait until Sunday. He is going to preach a barn burner! The people will be shouting in the aisles. Then Sunday comes. When he preaches, the fire does not burn. The ideas that so stirred him and excited him during preparation are now dull and lifeless. Ideas that leaped with life are now limp. The content of the sermon is there, but there is no life, no lift, no leap.

What went wrong? Probably, the preacher did not understand the mental processes involved in vitalizing his sermon during delivery. Though his sermon was alive during its preparation, he failed to bring the sermon to life again for his people. The purpose of this chapter is to help you learn to get your sermon from the study to the pulpit without losing its life and dynamic. What I am trying to say in this chapter is, Sermons must not only be born; they must be born again. Steps must be taken in the time of preparation and just prior to delivery to ensure that the sermon comes alive again in the mind and the heart of the preacher.

Steps to Vitalization

Several factors in the matter of sermon preparation come to bear upon mental vitalization at the moment of delivery. Alexander Maclaren placed an empty chair before him as he prepared his sermons. That empty chair represented to him the people in his congregation who would listen to him preach his sermon. The chair was a constant reminder to him that his sermons were being prepared for real people. Although Maclaren's method may not appeal to you or be practical, always be aware you are preparing the truths of Scripture to be delivered to *people*. Old people concerned with health and dying will be listening to you. Busy men will be there, taking time from the hectic pace of the daily business world. Young people, who are dealing with peer pressure and making crucial decisions in life, will be listening to what you say. Keep them in mind as you study the Scriptures to prepare your sermons.

As you put your message together, constantly keep in mind the importance of applying the timeless truths of Scripture to the pressing needs of people today. Be constantly asking yourself, So what? What does this have to do with my people? Make your illustrations and applications understandable to your people. Many preachers lose vitality in their sermons because they do not relate to the common experiences of their people.

The method of sermon delivery you choose will also influence your ability to make your sermon come alive. I question the method of reading it from a manuscript. Some men are able to read in such a way that the truths they read are alive and powerful. Most cannot. My observation is that usually such delivery *sounds* like it is being read. That is fatal to good communication in the pulpit.

I do not recommend that you memorize your sermon. To memorize a sermon word for word removes from vocal communication the vital elements of spontaneity and freshness. A memorized sermon sounds just that—memorized. As we shall see, certain key elements of the sermon may be memorized. We are not primarily concerned in this kind of memorization with the ability to recall exact words, however. The focus is rather upon the central thoughts and ideas to be conveyed.

Sermon delivery is alive and vital to its finest degree when it is extemporaneous. By extemporaneous I do not mean impromptu. Extemporaneous sermons are delivered on the basis of the most careful and thorough preparation.

How may the preacher preach extemporaneously in a way that makes his sermon come to life in the consciousness of his hearers? He must be able to remember what he has studied in a real and dynamic way. In this sense, Rahskoph's definition of memory is appropriate. He says: "Memory is the process by which past learning becomes effective in the present."[1] The three main phases in this process are: learning, retention, and recall.

Several laws of learning may be employed. The law of *frequency* has to do with the relation between the number of times one practices going over the material and the amount of the material that is remembered. The preacher should go over his material many times. Frequency of contact with the material will place the basic concepts firmly in his mind.

The law of *recency* is also important. This law has to do with the time the material is gone over. The preacher should go over his sermon notes on Saturday night and again on Sunday morning.

There is also the law of *intensity* or vividness. This law means that the preacher must place strong mental energy in his learning effort. His best mental abilities must be focused intense-

1. Horace G. Rahskoph, *Basic Speech Improvement* (New York: Harper & Row, 1965), p. 201.

ly and with all clarity upon his material.

The second phase in preparation for extemporaneous delivery is retention. By retention I mean preserving what you have learned during a latent period. Frequency of repetition of what you have learned will greatly aid your retention. Obviously, the preacher does not have time to go over his material in the moments right before he stands to preach. But he can go over the material before that point, and the number of times he does so will greatly enhance his powers of retention.

The third phase in this kind of preparation for delivery is recall. The preacher will have so thoroughly assimilated the contents of the message that he can recall them with clarity and vividness. The idea is to reconstruct not simply the words but the actual concepts and principles of his sermon that will enable the words to flow smoothly.[2]

Let me make some further suggestions about how to master your sermon material. First, so deepen your understanding of your material that you thoroughly know what you are saying. Second, have strong organization for what you want to say. Third, understand the logical relationships of the ideas in your message. Know how the various ideas in your sermon fit together.

Fourth, rehearse the thought sequences of your sermon. Think them through one by one. Speak them out loud. Master the ideas and pictures of your sermon. Depend upon logical rather than verbal memory. Doing this will enable you to recall your message much easier. You will be surprised at how many actual phrases and word sequences will come back to you when you know thoroughly the logical sequence of your concepts. When you are not trying so hard to remember the words, they will flow much better. Words cluster better around ideas and pictures than they do around attempts to memorize them.[3]

Fifth, distribute your study over several different times. That is why I recommend you study on Saturday night and then early Sunday morning as well.

2. Ibid., pp. 202-3.
3. Donald Demaray, *An Introduction to Homiletics* (Grand Rapids: Baker, 1974), p. 138.

Finally, overlearn your material. Be so familiar with what you are going to say that it is a part of you.

Thus far we have spent most of our attention on getting your sermon material prepared for the moment of delivery. Now let us consider how you may prepare *yourself* for the moment of delivery. In general, the preacher's habits of observation must be strengthened. The preacher must work to increase his powers of imagination. These matters were discussed in the previous chapter. General preparation should be done constantly. These matters must become a way of life to the preacher.

Specific preparation has to do with those steps the preacher takes to get himself ready to deliver a specific message. The sermon must actually be worked into the mind and heart of the preacher. McFarland says: "What is in the well of your heart will show up in the bucket of your speech."[4] That is another way of saying that good expression depends upon good impression. Whatever the materials the preacher may use in his sermon, they must become real to him. If the sermon is not real and alive to the preacher as he delivers it, there is little chance of its being real to the congregation. Robinson says: "An audience senses when a preacher reads words from the wall of his mind. Let a preacher agonize with thought and words at his desk, and what he writes will be internalized."[5]

The preacher is not called upon to preach only original thoughts; he is not forbidden to use the thoughts and ideas he gleans from others. But those thoughts must be made a part of his own thinking and feeling. Many preachers borrow thoughts from others, but never digest them in their own minds by reflection and meditation. As a result, they are not internalized. The preacher must live the truths of the sermon he is preparing. The sermon must be preached to himself before it is preached to others.

4. Kenneth McFarland, *Eloquence in Public Speaking* (Englewood Cliffs, N.J.. Prentice-Hall, 1961), p. 49.
5. Haddon W. Robinson, *Biblical Preaching* (Grand Rapids: Baker, 1980), p. 178.

The Intellectual and Emotional Modes

At this point we should consider the two modes we use as we preach, the intellectual and the emotional. The intellectual mode is the language of the mind. This mode is expressed by the words we use. If done well, the specific words used in sermon delivery will convey adequate intellectual content so that the listeners will be able to comprehend what the preacher is saying. But the preacher also speaks in the emotional mode, the language of the feelings. The emotional mode is expressed by the way the words are said, muscle tensions, and the overall mood created in delivery. I am not referring here to emotional preaching. Rather, I am talking about the overall emotional communication that comes from within the deepest feelings of the preacher himself. Stevenson and Diehl have pointed out there are two levels of emotion expressed in the delivery of a sermon. *Pathos* refers to the preacher's attitude toward himself and others. This is the deepest level of the preacher's emotions. On the other hand, *melism* has to do with the preacher's immediate feelings about the particular sermon he is to deliver. All of us are more interested in some subjects than others. Our attitude toward the sermon will be communicated as we preach. If I am alive to my sermon, my sermon will be alive to me. When the intellectual mode and the emotional mode cooperate with one another, the message is delivered with a great deal of effectiveness. When the emotional mode contradicts the intellectual mode, the emotional message is more readily accepted by the listeners than the intellectual.[6] The preacher may have the right message, but the way he handles his message may cause his listeners to reject it.

That is the reason some preachers are able to preach on stern, negative subjects, yet receive a favorable response from the listeners. Other preachers may preach upon positive subjects, yet create a negative response. If the preacher conveys through the emotional mode a sense of empathy with the people, they are much more likely to respond to him favorably. The preacher

---

6. Al Fasol, "A Guide to Improving Your Preaching Delivery" (Southwestern Baptist Theological Seminary, Ft. Worth, Tex. (Mimeographed), p. 8.

may say nearly anything he wants to say to the people if they are convinced he loves them, is interested in them, and wants to help them.

The preacher should search his inmost heart about his deepest attitudes. He should ask himself these questions: How do I feel toward this message? What do I feel toward myself? What are my feelings toward the audience? If the answers to these questions are not good, the preacher needs to do some heart searching before he delivers his message.[7]

Some specific work on the sermon on Saturday night or early Sunday morning will enable you to preach the sermon in a more effective way. The preacher should take some time to look again at the sermon as a whole. What is the overall purpose of the message? What does he want to accomplish? These considerations must be clearly in mind as he looks to the time of sermon delivery.

Take time to master the contents of the sermon. In addition to the sermon notes I prepare for filing purposes, I also prepare preaching notes. Normally these are written out by hand. They are as simple as possible. The key words of the sermon outline are included. Certain quotations and essential data in the sermon are also included. During this specific sermon preparation time I try to relive each part of the sermon in my imagination. I try to make the thoughts of the sermon as vivid as possible. I visualize the mental pictures in my message. For more abstract concepts, I try to imagine pictures that will easily convey to me the meaning. For instance, if I am talking in terms of progress, I may think in terms of a train moving along the track, making progress from station to station. If I am discussing liberty, I may picture the Statue of Liberty or a liberated slave. This enables abstract concepts in my sermon to come alive in my imagination.

After I have gone over each part of my sermon, attempting to live it out in my imagination, I speak the sermon to imagined hearers. I check the way I say certain parts of the sermon. Does it sound right? Will this make the maximum impact upon those

7. Dwight E. Stevenson and Charles F. Diehl, *Reaching People from the Puplit* (Grand Rapids: Baker, 1958), p. 74.

who hear it? Then, in imagination, I become several of my prospective hearers. I try to imagine how they would respond to this particular sermon. This procedure enables me to make the sermon real in my own soul.

Another helpful procedure to follow in preparing to deliver the sermon is to pray the message to the Lord. On your knees, in the presence of the Lord, go over each part of your sermon. Can you ask the approval of the Lord on what you are going to say? Is the sermon pleasing to Him? This is a helpful step as you prepare to preach.

The Moment of Delivery

We come now to the actual moment of delivery. You have taken the steps of specific preparation. The message is alive to you. You have prepared, you have prayed, you have internalized the sermon. Now you stand before your waiting congregation. If your sermon is to be effective as you deliver it, you must actually experience what you are saying as you say it. What you visualize you must now vitalize.

Your sermon must come from within. When you have prepared your sermon and placed it in some kind of written form, it becomes external to you. On paper the sermon has an existence of its own. Therefore, during the time of specific preparation the sermon must be born again in your heart. You must get the reality of the sermon back into your very being. I do not mean to belabor this point. I am simply trying to reinforce the importance of your sermon actually coming from within you. This is what the older preachers meant when, at the conclusion of the message, they said: "Brethren, I have delivered my soul to you this morning."

The sermon will be alive as you deliver it if you have a definite desire to share its contents with your people. A sermon must never become a soliloquy. Too often preachers deliver a sermon as if it were a work of art. They seem to be delivering it for its own sake, to be preaching it only to themselves. Because they have focused so much on the sermon, they have forgotten that the sermon was prepared to be delivered to a congregation.

When preachers do that, their attention is turned away from the people. They have poor eye contact, and they are unaware of the reaction of their listeners. As a result, they are unable to adjust their delivery to the changing reactions of the congregation.

Failure of this sort is only avoided when the preacher has a sincere desire to communicate God's truth to the people. If this desire is present, the preacher will use as many ways as he can possibly bring to his command to convey his message. A doctor who wants to warn his patient to quit smoking will draw upon all his knowledge of the dangers of smoking, will use every potential danger smoking may create, will paint every dark picture he can paint to warn the patient against smoking. The same is true of the pastor who earnestly desires to convey the great truths of the Bible to his people.

How can a preacher develop this sincere desire to share his sermon with others? He must remember his calling to preach. Let him go back to the time when the call of God first came upon his soul with force and freshness. All of the emotions and high aspirations that filled his being at that time must be made to live in his soul again. He must place himself where the people sit. He must be aware of all the different ages represented in his congregation. He must become aware of the problems, the burdens, the heartaches, the hopes and aspirations of his people.

He must keep his heart warm and receptive to God. If the preacher is spiritually vital, his sermons will also be vital. Thus, it is most important that a preacher maintain a daily devotional life. Through reading the Bible and daily contact with God in prayer, the preacher will keep himself in a position to be God's effective spokesman to men.

During the delivery of the sermon the preacher must see each idea as he presents it. The ideas must actually come alive in his mind. He must see all he possibly can by means of his imagination. Imagination has previously been described as the ingredient that makes the difference between a good preacher and a poor preacher. The preacher should allow his imagination to work freely on the pictures his sermon contents provide to his mind.

Give your hearers as many intellectual and emotional stimuli as you can find to make your sermon alive to them. They will be able by means of their imaginations to see, hear, touch, taste, and smell what you are talking about. Perhaps you are describing the cross. As the scene comes alive in your own mind, based on your previous preparation and the exercise of your emotion, express what you see to your listeners. Do not let mental laziness cause you to think of how you saw the cross in your preparation. See the scenes of Calvary during the actual moment of delivery. If you can recreate these images in the minds of your listeners as you preach, they will be stirred and moved by what you say.

I will have more to say about the importance of audience reaction in the section on the psychological aspects of delivery, but here let me say, watch the reactions of your people. Look at them while you deliver your sermon. Their reaction will let you know whether or not they are with you and understand what you say. See individuals as you speak.

Be sure to use a proper amount of emotional support for the things you say. By means of word color, gesture, and bodily tensions you can support the intellectual content of your sermon. That will enable your message to be more than an intellectual presentation of a series of thoughts and ideas. Through this method of sermon delivery you actually "flesh out" the truths of your sermon.

Preaching with mental vitalization relieves you of the necessity of concentrating upon how to use the vocal means of expression. While you are delivering your sermon you do not have to be overly concerned about the mechanics of delivery. You are master of your material instead of its mastering you. The contents of the material then dictate to the vocal mechanism how you say what you say.

Such delivery will have a positive effect on your listeners. Your message will be intense, compelling, captivating, and convincing. Such a delivery will result in a conversational style of speaking. I refer to conversational in the highest sense of the word, not merely to someone's standing in a pulpit and talking in a calm manner. It will be interesting to the listeners. The result will be delivery that is unusually compelling.

Let me summarize: See what you say. This is mental visualization. A sermon must not only be born; it must be born again. This is mental visualization.

PART 3

Rhetorical Aspects of Sermon Delivery

In recent years there has been a tendency to disparage rhetorical studies as they relate to sermon delivery. Few textbooks on the subject give much help in this area. Rhetoric, generally defined, is the art of using words effectively in speaking to influence or persuade others. This is certainly a legitimate area of study for the preacher who desires to preach effectively. The obvious dangers involved in rhetorical study must not cause us to fail to investigate this area of sermon delivery.

Broadus mentions rhetoric in his classic *Preparation and Delivery of Sermons.* He defines rhetoric as the art of ready utterance, appropriate expression, and moving appeal.[1] There are some dangers to the study of rhetoric. Too much attention to rules and norms for delivery can produce a rigidity in one's delivery. There is also the danger that too much attention to the art of rhetoric can produce a kind of unreality about your preaching. The goal is to be yourself. Preach in your natural voice, utilizing your own personality. You desire to improve so that you are the very best you are capable of becoming. To this end an understanding of the rhetorical aspects of sermon delivery can assist you.

Three main areas are considered in this section. First is a chapter on the use of words. The preacher must understand the

---

1. John A. Broadus, *The Preparation and Delivery of Sermons* (New York: Harper, 1926), p. 9.

difference between using words in oral style and using them in written style. Guidelines will be given to help you learn to select words that will be the most effective as you preach.

There is a chapter on the techniques of persuasion. The preacher indeed is a persuader. That cannot be avoided. We will study methods that are ethical and acceptable in the call for a response to the gospel. I especially hope you will profit from the chapter on preaching and the techniques of drama. Preachers must learn to use dramatic technique in their preaching. Too many preachers deal with truth in an unemotional, unexciting manner. Learning some of the ways to present your sermon dramatically will greatly strengthen your sermon delivery.

9

The Use of Words

The preacher speaks the Word of God in the words of men. As the preacher seeks to convey what God is saying he must do so in language that is clear and understandable. Therefore, the man of God who would be an effective communicator must give attention to the use of words in his sermon delivery.

The power of words cannot be overestimated. Julius Caesar is reported to have said: "The choice of words is the source of eloquence." Joseph Conrad said: "Give me the right word and the right accent and I will move the world."[1] The preacher may greatly enhance or tragically weaken the effectiveness of his message by his choice of words.

In one sense the effective preacher must be an artist. Such an art may not be reduced to a step-by-step formula. There are, however, several useful guidelines. His words must be clear, interest-provoking, and forceful.

Oral Style Versus Written Style

We must be aware that there is a significant difference between the oral use of words and the written use of words. This touches on the matter of style. The writer has an advantage in that written words may be seen by the eyes of the reader. On the other hand, the oral communicator must use words that can be understood at the moment of hearing by his listeners.

1. In Horace G. Rahskoph, *Basic Speech Improvement* (New York: Harper & Row, 1965), p. 318.

Spoken style must be instantly intelligible to the hearer. The reader may pause to ponder the meaning of a word used by a particular author. The listener is not given this luxury. He must understand in an instant what is being said by the speaker.

Also, spoken style must make more use of suspense and climax. A reader is able to look at the previous sentences and even anticipate the words to follow. That is not as possible for the listener. Therefore, the preacher must use words that build a sense of expectancy. Similarly, spoken style requires more repetition and restatement. On the pages of a book words may be stated and left for themselves. In spoken style the preacher must be careful to ensure that his listeners have clearly heard what he wants to say.

Spoken style must use more objective elements of vividness. For this reason a preacher's sermon should have more comparisons, for the listeners must be able to understand what is being said on the basis of comparisions with ideas and concepts that are familiar to them. In spoken style more use of contrast should be made. The preacher must use figurative language to produce pictures in the minds of the listeners. Spoken English must also include more questions and personal elements of address. The preacher must use words that create a sense of rapport with the audience.

Also, spoken style, because it must be vivid, makes more frequent use of illustrations. Illustrations are often remembered longer than any other part of the sermon. In selecting his sermon contents the preacher should keep that in mind. Using good illustrations and including interesting stories is a vital part of good sermon delivery.

Spoken style has more of an eagerness about it. The writer of a book has the advantage that, under normal circumstances, the reader brings to his book some initial interest. The author is not faced with the need to create as much interest on the part of the reader as the preacher must on the part of his listeners. For this reason, the preacher's sermon must be delivered in words that convey excitement, interest, expectancy, and eagerness.

Spoken style needs a sense of rhythm and smoothness. In effective sermon delivery the words selected should glide easily on the preacher's lips and fall pleasantly upon the listener's ears. Some combinations of words are difficult to articulate smoothly. For this reason, the preacher will do well to experiment with different ways of saying what he wants to say. For instance, "John the Baptist taught repentence" is harder to say smoothly than is "John the Baptizer taught repentance." The latter expression removes the problem of using a word that ends with a *t* just before a word that begins with *t*.

This chapter is not intended to be an instant solution to the matter of good oral style. Rather, the suggestions are intended to point to the kinds of words that are likely to make your sermon delivery more effective.

Appropriate Word

First, use words appropriate to the occasion. You must be keenly aware of the occasion, the audience, and the type of message to be delivered. Choose a level of vocabulary fitting the time, place, and purpose of the gathering. Normally, you will be preparing a sermon to be delivered to your congregation on Sunday. In that setting you must know your congregation. Choose words that can best relate to your people. Do not make the mistake of bringing the technical terminology you learned in college or seminary to the pulpit. Although the words may sound impressive, they will not likely communicate effectively to plain, hard-working people. Your purpose is not to be impressive. It is to communicate. Use one level of word selection for a sermon to children or young people and another level for a speech to the senior adults' group.

Simple Words

Words do not have to be long and complicated to be effective. Notice how short are the immortal words: "Four score and seven years ago"; "The Lord is my Shepherd"; "To be or not to be"; "We have nothing to fear but fear itself." A study of the sermons of Dwight L. Moody revealed that approximately 79 percent of the words he used were of one syllable. Sixteen percent were two syllables. Only 4 percent were three syllables.[2] That is undoubtedly the reason the common people of Moody's day heard him gladly. The preacher should think with the theologians and scholars but talk to the common man.

My intention has always been to preach so that the children in the congregation can easily understand what I am saying. I consider the greatest compliment I ever receive to be when a mother says to me, "Billy likes to hear you preach because he can understand what you say." When the little children can understand the words I use, I do not wonder if the grownups can. Martin Luther said: "A preacher should have the skill to teach the unlearned simply, roundly and plainly; for teaching is of more importance than exhorting. When I preach I regard neither doctors nor magistrates, of whom I have about forty in the congregation. I have all my eyes on the servant maids and the children. If the learned men are not well pleased with what they hear, well, the door is open."[3]

The American government is famous for the complexity of its directives. The rule seems to be, Never use a hundred words if a thousand will do. The delightful story is told of the plumber who wrote a government bureau in Washington that he had discovered clogged drains could be cleared by using hydrochloric acid. The bureau wrote back: "The efficacy of hydrochloric acid is indisputable, but the corrosive residue is incompatible with metallic permanence." How much easier it would have been for them to say: "Don't use hydrochloric acid. It messes up the pipes."[4]

Some would use the need for plain language as a reason not to use unfamiliar Bible terminology. That is not my purpose in recommending the use of simple words. When did an unbelieving world ever understand Bible language? The words of the Bible are special to those who know and love the gospel. The Bible

2. Kenneth McFarland, *Eloquence in Public Speaking* (Englewood Cliffs, N.J.: Prentice-Hall, 1961), p. 78.
3. In D. Martyn Lloyd-Jones, *Preaching and Preachers* (Grand Rapids: Zondervan, 1971), p. 129.
4. McFarland, p. 80.

preacher has the responsibility to teach the people the meaning of Bible terms. This may be done, however, in words that are simple and easy to understand.

Clear Words

Learn to use clear words. Strive for accuracy. Use words that give your meaning correctly. Avoid words that can refer to a variety of qualities or feelings. Such words as *nice, wonderful, terrific, fine, cute,* and *pretty* say little. There is power in the specific. Your words will have more weight when you say, "Way-cross, Georgia," instead of "a small southern town." To say, "A fox terrier chased the boy" is clearer than to say, "A dog chased the boy."

Clear words make the sermon easier for people to understand. To an amazing degree, people do misunderstand what preachers are trying to say. Preachers are often amazed at what some people think they heard them say. Clear words will lessen the degree of misunderstanding. At the outbreak of the Franco-Prussian War a general said to his officers, "Remember, gentlemen, that any order that can be misunderstood will be misunderstood."[5]

Emphatic Words

The preacher should use emphatic words. That does not mean that he should use superlatives indiscreetly. Rather, he should use strong words and employ repetition effectively. The preacher should avoid unnecessary qualifiers and should place the emphasis where it should be by judicious choice of words. Not all thoughts are of equal importance. The preacher ought to be sure to stress the truly important things. The big things in his sermon should be really big. The things that ought to be emphasized should be emphasized. That can be done in several ways. One way to emphasize words is by their place in the sentence.

5. In Josh McDowell, "Syllabus on Communication and Persuasion" (© Josh McDowell, 1983. Mimeographed), p. 2.

Normally, putting a word at the beginning or the end of a sentence emphasizes it.

The preacher can emphasize a particular thought by the amount of time he devotes to it. He can do this by reiteration— piling on facts. Restatement often indicates emphasis. He can also use repetition. He can say certain words or phrases over again and again until they are given strong emphasis. But let me warn you that repetition can be overdone. Too much restatement or repetition becomes tiresome and actually lessens the emphasis intended.

Some words reduce the emphasis of what is being said. Often called throwaway words, they are seen frequently in the Scriptures. For instances, in Luke 2:10 we read: "Fear not: for, behold, I bring you good tidings of great joy, which shall be to all people." To place the emphasis upon "behold" is to give wrong emphasis to the sentence. It actually takes away from what the sentence is intending to convey. Other such throwaway words are *and, for,* and *saying.* To emphasize these words is to throw off balance the intended meaning of what you say. Use strong nouns and verbs. Avoid overworked words and hackneyed expressions.

Nuance Words

A nuance word is one that is picture-building in nature. The word enables the listener to see what is being said. An Arab proverb puts it quite well: "He is the best speaker who can turn the ear into an eye."[6] Man's mind is more like an art museum than a chalkboard. The preacher who would communicate adequately to his listeners must use words that have sensory appeal. The sounds of words are important in transmitting your message. The combination of the sounds of vowels and consonants to help achieve a particular affect is called tone color.[7] For this reason, some prefer to use the term *color words.*

6. In Donald Demaray, *An Introduction to Homiletics* (Grand Rapids: Baker, 1974), p. 107.
7. Charlotte I. Lee and Frank Galati, *Oral Interpretation* (Boston: Houghton Mifflin, 1977), p. 215.

Pictures painted in the mind move people. We are aware that one picture is worth a thousand words. Let us not forget, however, that we can use words to paint powerful mental pictures. Jesus did that. He used words that called images to mind. He talked about seed sown in the soil; He spoke of a treasure hid in the field; He spoke of tares sown among wheat. Use words to help your listener call to his mind the same image you have in yours. Listen for the sound-suggestiveness of words. Speak of the *hum* of bees, the *thud* of the leg, the *buzz* of flies, the *moaning* of the wind. In listening to words you will notice that the actual difference in sound conveys the meaning of the word. The word *smooth* is slow and quiet. The word *sharp* is abrupt and to the point like a knife. Think of the words *slow* and *swift, bright* and *drab, crisp* and *soggy, gloomy* and *radiant*. What images do they paint in your mind?[8]

Work to speak in the language of pictures. Try your best to lay aside words that are colorless and abstract. Good preachers help people actually to live out what they are saying. They portray the truth with such vividness that the people feel as if they themselves are actually involved in what is going on.

Few Words

Use as few words as possible. There should be only enough repetition to adequately convey the point. Beyond this the people will become bored. Select words carefully with a definite purpose in mind. Be very careful about using superlatives carelessly. Some preachers toss words around so freely there is nothing left to be used when something really big is to be described. Certain words probably should be used very sparingly. The good preacher will rarely use such words as *colossal, thrilling, exciting, amazing, wonderful, splendid, worthwhile.*

Other preachers seem to be afflicted with "elegantitis." They are not able to use simple, clear, to-the-point words. Instead of saying, "go to bed," they speak of "retiring." Rather than "get-

8. Winston E. Jones, *Preaching and the Dramatic Arts* (New York: Macmillan, 1948), p. 68.

ting up" in the morning, they "rise." They do not "eat"; they "dine." Such words do not add to effective communication.

Jay Adams suggests that certain forms of word wax should be removed. Remove unnecessary superlatives from your speech. Eliminate trite and stale words. People get tired of hearing the same words over and over again. Do your best to cut out certain phrases that have a way of sticking in the preacher's vocabulary. Also, Adams suggests, refrain from using the additives *such as, and so forth,* and *in the next place.* These words contribute nothing to what is being said. He further suggests that you should avoid weasel words. They are words that unnecessarily qualify what you say. Eliminate run-on sentences. Learn to use an abundance of periods in your speaking.[9] A lasting, unforgettable impression can be made in a few words. The model prayer contains only 56 words. Lincoln's Gettysburg Address has only 266 words. The Declaration of Independence is only 300 words in length. Contrast this to a government order setting the price of cabbage that had 26,922 words![10]

Word Combinations

Give attention to the way words are put together. Some words fit together. Other words do not. When words clash there is difficulty in understanding. Keep your sentences short. Demaray points out that sentences averaging eleven words are easily understood by eighty-six percent of American adults. Seventeen words per average sentence will normally communicate with seventy-five percent of the American adults. More difficult speech, which contains twenty-nine or more words in a typical sentence, will communicate with only four and a half percent of the average audience.[11]

Actually there should be variety in your sentences. Do not allow your sentences to get into any kind of pattern Vary the

---

9. Jay Adams, *Pulpit Speech* (Phillipsburg, N.J.: Presbyterian and Reformed, 1971), p. 123.
10. Demaray, p. 131.
11. Ibid., pp. 132-33.

length and type of your sentences. That will help you maintain high interest on the part of your people and will create in them a sense of expectancy and suspense.

Obviously, the preacher cannot begin at once to be a master in his use of words. But there are several ways the preacher can begin immediately to increase his effectiveness in the use of words. He can be constantly enriching his vocabulary. He can study the dictionary. The plot will be boring, but he will increase his word power! He can listen to effective speakers, both preachers and otherwise, and note the words they use. He can increase his own store of picture-building words. He can observe words used by the great writers. The works of Charles Dickens and other master authors are especially helpful in learning to use words effectively.

The preacher must also know the local connotations of the words he uses. Those connotations will affect how the people receive what he says. If the words he uses are understood by his listeners in the way he understands them, he will be able to communicate effectively.

10

The Techniques of Persuasion

The preacher, in the finest sense of the term, is a persuader. Many of the older textbooks on preaching had a great deal to say about persuasion as a part of sermon preparation and delivery. This is true of the classic work on preaching by Dr. Broadus. In more recent years the homiletical writers have devoted little attention to matters of persuasion.

Perhaps the reason persuasion is more likely to be ignored today is that people are persuaded on the basis of different considerations these days. The more lengthy and technical arguments do not seem to move people to action in the twentieth century as they did in previous generations. Whitsell is probably quite correct when he says that people now are swayed more by illustrations, humor, and emotion than by sober argument.[1]

Still, there is a vital place for understanding the techniques of persuasion in effective pulpit communication. By persuasion I mean all ethical methods the preacher may use in his preaching to induce people to make the right decisions and do the right things. The sermons in the New Testament include many techniques of persuasion. The New Testament preachers preached for a verdict. Their intent was to bring their listeners to a point of decision that would eternally change their destiny. Their purpose was not merely the influencing of behavior, but ultimately the changing of character.

---

1. Farris D. Whitsell, *Power in Expository Preaching* (Old Tappan, N.J.: Revell, 1963), p. 63.

Advertising Appeals

The four basic methods of persuasion used in the field of advertising are well-known. These devices are very simple. First, there is the appeal to *virtue*. This device associates the product in question with all a person may regard as good and desirable. We are urged to buy a certain brand of soap because it will make us smell good. We cannot be without the latest toothpaste because it will give us sex appeal. Such a device calls attention to the person's interest in some desirable, achievable goal.

Second is the *poison* device. The one who would persuade associates failure to use the "desirable" product with everything people consider to be objectionable and harmful. If you do not use a certain shampoo, you will have dandruff. In turn, that dandruff will make you unappealing to members of the opposite sex. Therefore, you must purchase the new shampoo.

Third is the *testimonial*. This approach seeks to induce us to accept or reject a product on the basis of persons with reputation and personal appeal. Certain brands of cereal are to be eaten because sports heroes eat them. If you really want to be a hero, you will eat this particular brand.

The fourth device combines the other three to operate by means of group pressure. In terms of modern advertising techniques these four devices are like four sides of a square within which all persuasion is contained.[2]

From the perspective of the Christian preacher, how are these techniques of persuasion to be viewed? Obviously, certain aspects of these devices play a part in the preacher's role as a Christian persuader. But the preacher must remember that he is not merely involved in influencing behavior. His goal is to influence character and change destinies. The techniques of persuasion the preacher employs must be in keeping with larger, more complex, and nobler purposes. As the preacher stands before a congregation, with the Bible in his hand, in the power of the Holy Spirit, his motivation is to bring people to a life-changing experience with Christ. That is no small task. He must penetrate

2. Winston E. Jones, *Preaching and the Dramatic Arts* (New York: Macmillan, 1948), p. 39.

defenses, break down patterns of thought, and bring about changes in the lives of those who listen to him. The preacher's goal is this: that the minds of those who listen be convinced, that their emotions be stirred, and that their wills be activated.

Bible Persuasion

There are some who question the validity of the preacher's using any techniques of persuasion at all. Is there a moral and ethical basis for the use of persuasive techniques? Unfortunately, some within the ranks of the Christian ministry have become more like manipulators than persuaders. They have taken the attitude: "I don't care what method I use, just so it brings people to Christ. If it works, then fine. The end justifies the means." The fallacy of this kind of reasoning is that it equates being effective with being ethical. To take the position that any method of influence is good if it has positive results is open to challenge.

But there is adequate Bible basis for persuasion. A study of Paul's ministry reveals that he was a Christian persuader in the finest sense of the term. Just a few references to his preaching on his various missionary journeys will reveal this aspect of his ministry. In Acts 13:43 we are told that Paul spoke to Christian converts and "persuaded them to continue in the grace of God." In Corinth Paul preached in the synagogue every Sabbath and "persuaded the Jews and the Greeks" (Acts 18:4). As he stood before King Agrippa he said, "For I am persuaded that none of these things are hidden from him [King Agrippa]" (Acts 26:26). Other references might be cited. Paul brings the whole matter of persuasion as a part of sermon delivery into focus when he says: "Knowing therefore the terror of the Lord, we persuade men; but we are made manifest unto God; and I trust also are made manifest in your consciences" (2 Cor. 5:11). The particular word used in this passage means to persuade or to induce one by words to believe.[3]

Persuasion is what preaching is all about. The whole exist-

3. Joseph Henry Thayer, *Greek-English Lexicon* (Grand Rapids: Zondervan, 1963), p. 497.

ence and purpose of the sermon is to persuade. It moves the
souls of men. Therefore, the preacher will do well to develop and
train himself in the techniques of persuasion. He must do so,
however, with the purest motives in his heart. Again, Paul summarizes quite well when he says:

> For our exhortation was not of deceit, nor of uncleanness, nor in
> guile; but as we were allowed of God to be put in trust with the
> gospel, even so we speak; not as pleasing men, but God, which
> trieth our hearts. For neither at any time used we flattering words,
> as ye know, nor a cloak of covetousness; God is witness: nor of
> men sought we glory, neither of you, nor yet of others, when we
> might have been burdensome, as the apostles of Christ. But we
> were gentle among you, even as a nurse cherisheth her children: so
> being affectionately desirous of you, we were willing to have
> imparted unto you, not the gospel of God only, but also our own
> souls because ye were dear unto us. (1 Thessalonians 2:3-8)

Wrong Approaches

We must be persuaders, not manipulators. There are many
faulty approaches to persuasion. The first of these is to say, "I
won't try to persuade at all." This position is untenable for the
sincere Christian. The Christian is commanded by the Lord Jesus
Christ Himself to win men. For this reason, he cannot refuse his
responsibility to persuade others.

Neither can he look upon a person as just another scalp on
the belt or notch on the gun. This form of manipulation merely
uses people as part of a numbers game. The preacher must never
seek to persuade others in order to make himself appear to be
successful.

Still another approach is: "Show them only the silver lin-
ing." Shading the truth and failure to present the total picture is
sometimes seen in the testimonies of the successful, the famous,
or the beautiful who have become Christians. The impression is
given that to come to Christ will make a person one or all of
these things. Such a method of persuasion is untrue to the Christian gospel. Very often to become a Christian means the wealthy
may no longer be as wealthy. The famous may lose their fame.
Methods of manipulation that promise worldy success are un-

worthy of the sincere Christian preacher who desires to bring men to faith in Christ and to a changed life-style.

As we learn the techniques of persuasion we must keep in mind the words of Paul: "But have renounced the hidden things of dishonesty, not walking in craftiness, nor handling the word of God deceitfully; but by manifestation of the truth commending ourselves to every man's conscience in the sight of God". (2 Cor. 4:2)

Ethos, Logos, Pathos

Aristotle's three factors in persuasion are familiar to most of us. The first he calls *ethos*. By this he means the impression the preacher himself makes upon his audience. The validity of what the preacher says is strengthened or weakened on the basis of the sincerity of the preacher himself. The preacher who preaches the Word of God to others must live the message he preaches. The people who listen to him must have the distinct impression that he practices what he preaches. A few years ago I had a sore throat and went to the drugstore to buy some throat medicine. The druggist sought to sell me a new brand. He was coughing so much himself, I was not interested in his cough medicine! Be what you are selling. The character of the preacher is crucial in the kind of reception his sermon will receive. If the listeners get the impression of modesty, sincerity, humility, and genuineness, they will be more likely to respond favorably to what he says.

Aristotle also talked about *logos*. This term refers to the use of logic and formal methods of persuasion. Evidently, logic and formal persuasion were prominent in the sermons of the apostle Paul. The elements of analogy, induction and deduction, and testimony are involved in these formal methods of argument.

Aristotle also referred to *pathos*. Pathos is the appeal to the emotions. Although we would never appeal to feelings exclusively, we must recognize there is a valid use of the emotional appeal. Quite often these appeals are more likely to move individuals in our society than the more formal ones. We must be careful not to appeal to baser motives but rather should appeal to the highest longings and aspirations of men.

Charles Koller mentions seven appeals to the heart: the

appeal to altruism (a benevolent regard for the interests of others), the appeal to aspiration (the universal hunger for spiritual happiness or a sense of completeness), the appeal to curiosity (susceptibility to that which appears novel, unfamiliar, or mysterious), the appeal to duty (the divine urge to do a thing because it is right or to refrain from a thing because it is wrong), the appeal to fear, the appeal to love, and the appeal to reason.[4]

On the basis of Aristotle's divisions we might say that persuasive techniques fall into three categories: personal appeal, logical argument, and emotional appeal.

Personal Appeal

There is always a persuasive element in personal testimony in preaching. The testimony of the preacher himself, if he is credible, will be a strong one. There is strength in the "satisfied customer." Paul used this approach when he said to King Agrippa, "I am persuaded" (Acts 26:26). Of course, the preacher cannot turn every sermon into a personal testimony. He may, however, include the testimony of others as well as his own. Personal accounts of answers to prayer, salvation experiences, and God's working in the lives of individuals can be used most effectively in sermons. A good store of information about Christian personalities throughout history and on the current scene can be used to persuade others.

Logical Argument

A variety of logical appeals may be used in persuading others. There is strong authority in the Word of God. The preaching of the Bible is accompanied by the authenticating testimony of the Holy Spirit in the hearts of those who listen. Billy Graham has been known throughout his ministry for his recurring statement, "The Bible says." Facts and statistics may be helpful in influencing people to make a desired commitment. Pack your

4. Charles W. Koller, *Expository Preaching Without Notes* (Grand Rapids: Baker, 1962), pp. 109-12.

sermons with helpful and supportive facts and statistics.

Anticipate and be prepared to answer objections that might arise in the minds of your listeners. In doing so, you will dampen the objector's gunpowder before it can be fired. But be sure not to raise objections the people who listen will not raise. Also, if you do raise objections, be sure you can intelligently handle them! If you are not on top of the material, your answers may be so weak you will accomplish the opposite of what you intend.

I have found that a well-organized sermon will be more persuasive than an unorganized one. The human mind thinks logically. If you are able to present your message in a clear, logical manner, there will be much more persuasiveness about it.

Emotional Appeal

Certain emotional appeals have great strength. The Christian life should be presented in such a positive way that the listeners should want to become Christians. Heaven should be made so appealing that any thinking person would want to go there. Learn to make the destiny of the human soul so vivid and compelling that the people will desire it. The psalmist put it quite well when he admonished: "O taste and see that the Lord is good" (Psalm 34:8). To create this type of response in an individual has within it the power to change character and create desire for a nobler life.

The appeal to fear is not an unworthy one. There has been a tendency in our time to minimize and even scoff at the appeals to fear preachers used to make. Of course, there must be no unreasonable or excessive use of fear. Scare tactics for the sake of fear itself are unwarranted. Yet fear is a real emotion of the human heart. The Bible presents in the plainest terms the dire consequences of the life that rejects Jesus Christ. Either we accept the Bible truth about these matters or we do not. If we do, then in faithfulness to the truth and love for those to whom we preach, we must give adequate warning. The doctor who seeks to cause his patient to abstain from smoking does not hesitate to use an appeal to fear. The Bible does still say: "It is a fearful thing to fall into the hands of the living God" (Hebrews 10:31).

The preacher may also use an appeal to love. In one sense all persuasion is an appeal to love—love of self, love of others, or love of God. We appeal to the Christians in our congregation on the basis of their love for Christ and desire to serve and please Him. We also appeal to all men that a response of love to Him is based upon His love for us. First John 4:19 says: "We love him because he first loved us." Paul said, "For the love of Christ constraineth us" (2 Cor. 5:14*a*).

Emory Griffin mentions role play as an effective means of persuasion. By this he means that the Christian persuader, for a few moments, ceases to be himself and adopts the view of the character he is portraying. This enables the persuader to create in the minds of his listeners certain desirable or undesirable mental pictures. By inducing our listeners to imaginatively share with us in a new position or pattern of thought, we stand a better chance of influencing them in that direction.[5] We have discussed in other sections of the book the uses of imagination in effective sermon delivery. The imagination is also a powerful persuader. By role play we can activate the imaginations of our listeners. If we can get our listeners to live out in their own imaginations the truths we are seeking to convey, we will be better able to change their attitudes and behavior.

The wise preacher will learn to use many of these techniques of persuasion. He will not rest his case with a single appeal. The preacher is wasting his time when he attempts to persuade people merely on the basis of obligation or duty. Scolding or fervent entreaty will benefit very little. But if the preacher uses a combination of persuasive techniques, he may be able to help those who listen to him see and feel for themselves something that is most desirable and worthwhile for their lives. The preacher will have accomplished his desired intention when his listeners join him in saying, "I am persuaded."

In closing this chapter I want to give a few general suggestions that will help you as you seek to win a hearing for what you say. The constitution guarantees you freedom of speech, but it does not guarantee you a listening audience. The right to be

5. Emory A. Griffin, *The Mind Changers* (Wheaton, Ill.: Tyndale, 1976), p. 82.

heard must be earned. First, be sure you know what you are talking about. This points us back to the importance of adequate sermon preparation. If you are poorly prepared, you will not have to tell your listeners. Lack of preparation is painfully and even disgustingly apparent. Those who listen have given you precious moments of their time. They have a right to know that you have prepared to the point that you are up on what you are speaking about. Know your subject.

Next, love your audience. If the preacher has feelings of hostility toward his people, they will immediately pick up on it. As you preach you must communicate to your people, more by manner and attitude than by words, that you really love them and care for them. Get to know your people. Spend as much time with them as you possibly can. The more we are around people the better chance there is they will respond favorably to us.

Do not be afraid to be open in your sermons. Let them know you are a real person. Admit your failures. People are more responsive to a person who conveys human warmth and reality.

11

Preaching and the Techniques of Drama

Probably no generation has experienced such a vociferous attack upon preaching as ours. For a few years there seemed to be no end of objection to the traditional sermon preached on Sunday morning. The thought was that preaching had outlived its usefulness, was not relevant to our day, and only served to bore those upon whom it was imposed. Obviously much of this criticism stemmed from a bias against the very nature of the Christian evangel itself. If there is a desire to eliminate the message of the gospel, what better way to do so than to silence its voice in the pulpit?

In all fairness, however, we must admit that some criticism against preaching has been due to the lack of interesting and stimulating pulpit delivery. All of us who have been brought up in the church know what it is to endure a dead, dry, *long* sermon. Dr. Broadus tells the homely story of a preacher who suggested to a sleepy hearer that snuff might keep him awake. The weary member replied: "Couldn't you put a little more snuff into your sermons?"[1]

The preacher can do much to relieve the problem of congregational boredom by understanding the role of dramatic technique in sermon delivery. Not that the preacher deals in unreal subject matter or that he merely acts out something that is not a

1. John A. Broadus, *The Preparation and Delivery of Sermons* (New York: Harper, 1926), p. 252.

genuine part of his own life. Rather, the preacher must employ dramatic techniques if he is to preach the meaning of his message in the most effective manner possible. That does not mean that preaching is an act the preacher puts on before a congregation. Something altogether different is intended.

From the viewpoint of the dynamics of speaking, sermon delivery may be viewed as a science. From the perspective of effective communication with a listening congregation, the preacher must be an artist. He must be an artist in his use of words, in his ability to use the principles of persuasion, and in his employment of dramatic techniques. The preacher must utilize all three elements if he is to effectively convey the great truths of the Bible. Haddon Robinson says: "While a preacher is more than an actor, he should not be less."[2]

The thesis of this chapter is that effective preaching must utilize the techniques of drama if it is to be all God intends it. The preacher's message may be well prepared. The points may proceed with the clearest possible logic. Sound principles may abound in the message. All of this is of little effect unless human life is touched. No message will exert lasting influence unless it comes to bear upon the emotional life of those who listen to it.

In one sense, listening to a sermon preached from the Bible is in itself an emotional experience. The preacher must never forget this. The old adage, A person changed against his will is of the same opinion still, is true. Logic and argument are only temporarily effective. Permanent change in the hearts of men can be accomplished only as the emotions are moved. What one feels about what is said is much more determinative than some may realize. Consequently, whether or not a sermon is accepted or rejected is often largely due to the emotions that are produced in regard to it.

The preacher is the controlling factor in the preaching situation. The architecture of the building, the makeup of the congregation, the song service, the general atmosphere of the speaking situation itself are all factors in the preaching event. But the key element is the preacher himself. The preacher must not only

2. Haddon W. Robinson, *Biblical Preaching* (Grand Rapids: Baker, 1980), p. 207.

convince the intellect, he must stir the emotions. This can be done most effectively when the preacher understands the techniques of drama.

The Dramatic Arts

The dramatic arts include those areas of human expression that are vivid, moving, and impelling. The preacher may learn from them how to more effectively convey the reality of his sermon. The dramatic arts recreate experiences in the minds of those who view them. For this reason all dramatic art gives a primary place to feeling. The artist releases a variety of feelings in those who behold his work of art. The same holds true for the preacher. By use of words he fulfills the function of an artist. Whereas the artist creates feelings with a canvas, the preacher does the same by his use of words. He stirs the imagination of those who listen to him. The preacher makes visible what is invisible for his congregation. He enables his listeners to receive information through vicarious experience.

The writer who effectively uses words enables his reader to go places he has never been before. By means of his skill in writing he enables the reader to sense how others must have felt even though they may have lived many miles away and long centuries before. The preacher does the same thing with oral words. As the preacher stirs the imagination of his listeners he brings home to them the meaning of events and experiences beyond the orbit of their lives. The preacher transmits information and insight from himself to his listeners by inducing imagined experience.

The preacher by means of dramatic technique gives his hearers an opportunity to react to life's situations in terms of their own emotions. He pictures vice in such a way as to make it ugly to those who practice it. He paints virtue so beautifully as to make it desirable even to those who do not possess it.

I am convinced that much modern preaching misses the mark due to the lack of the dramatic element in it. Life itself is drama. People are involved in dramatic situations daily. People are loving and hating. They are struggling and surviving. They are living and dying. Life is not dull and drab. For this reason, to preach truthfully is to preach dramatically.[3] We who preach God's living Word to living people must do so in terms of real life experience. We preach a book filled with the experiences of people who actually lived, spoke, struggled, and faced eternity. There is no reason the preacher should not be able to preach such a real book in a vivid, exciting manner. Painters do this for their viewers. They see the world around them. Then, through the medium of their own souls, they pour out on canvas for all the world to see. Why cannot the preacher do the same thing when he preaches?

Study the life and ministry of Jesus. In the grandest sense of the word, Jesus was a verbal artist. He enabled men to see truths and values they had long forgotten. As He moved among men, He stopped to observe playing children. From that point on His disciples saw children as they had never seen them before. He stopped to talk with a poor, outcast woman. Thereafter his disciples saw the hidden potential in the lowest of people. He stopped at the Temple treasury to view a poor, timid widow drop her two mites into the receptacle. From that day on the giving of the least to the Lord was sanctified and magnified in the minds of His disciples. He spoke of the lilies of the field and forever painted them with indelible strokes upon the minds of His followers. Why cannot you do the same in the delivery of your sermon?

Lorado Taft, the sculptor, called some friends to the porch of his summer home. He wanted to show them the sunset. The western sky was a panoply of shifting shapes and vivid colors. As his friends looked, Taft spoke of the beautiful variety of details and effects in the sunset. Those who listened to him saw more than they had ever seen before. A simple maid, serving refreshments, was unnoticed by sculptor and friends. "Mr. Taft," she suddenly said, "may I run down the road? I want to go home a minute."

"Why do you want to go home right now?"

"I want to show my mother the sunset," she exclaimed.

---

3. Winston E. Jones, *Preaching and the Dramatic Arts* (New York: Macmillan, 1948), p. 24.

"But, my dear, your mother has been living here many years. She has seen many sunsets."

The maid replied earnestly, "We never saw the sunsets here until you came."[4] By means of dramatic technique the preacher helps his people see what they never saw before.

In the remainder of the chapter I want to briefly discuss some aspects of dramatic technique as it applies to the delivery of a sermon.

Capture Attention

In chapter 13 more will be said concerning the attention span of the audience. But in this chapter let us simply assert that the preacher must be able to capture the attention of his listeners. If you fail to gain attention at the beginning, the difficulty of gaining attention at other points along the way is greatly increased. Every preacher should study the way a playwright designs his play. The playwright has an express purpose, an intended effect. The audience before whom the play will be given is always large in the design and fashion of the play. The preacher should arrange and build his sermons in the same manner. The people must be kept in mind throughout the preparation of his sermon.

Variety

A good play has a great deal of change, suspense, and surprise. The script is written to build to a definite climax. Throughout the play there will be alternating moods and differing rhythms of interest.[5] A preacher should prepare his sermon for delivery with the same kind of arrangement in mind: the sermon should include a great deal of variety. Preaching is often an intense matter. For this reason there must be variety and alteration in mood in the sermon. Neither the preacher nor his hearers can keep up to a high level of excitement for an extended period of time.[6]

4. Ibid., p. 28.
5. Ibid., p. 53.
6. Broadus, p. 252.

Effective Introductions

A sermon might be compared to a one-act play. Within a single span of time the play must present itself, move through its various ingredients, and come to conclusion. A sermon generally conforms to this pattern. But because the preacher does not have intermissions between his points, he must prepare his introduction with the definite purpose of securing and maintaining attention.

Long introductions are a waste of time. Regardless of the interest that may already be present in the hearers, a long introduction may actually dissipate that interest. Get to the thesis of your message soon. In the earlier years of my ministry I sometimes got so involved in the technicalities of my introduction I actually ran out of time before I could elaborate upon the main points of the message! Get to your point. Do it quickly.

A sameness of presentation greatly lessens the effect of an introduction. Avoid repetitious introductions. Do not begin every sermon by saying, "My subject this morning is. . ." or "As you will recall in our message last Sunday. . ." Variety in the introduction is important.

Development and Climax

The next step in presenting your sermon is the logical, orderly development of your theme. This theme should be developed throughout your message with a gradual heightening of interest. For that to be achieved, there must be constant movement throughout the message. Do not dwell upon any single point longer than is actually necessary. Sometimes you will discover you have lost your audience. Heads begin to move. There is whispering and moving around. If you will watch your sermon at that point you will often find you are saying over and over again what you have already made clear.[7]

A good drama has a distinct crescendo. The same is true of a sermon. Correctly done, a sermon will reach a climax in inter-

7. H. A. Overstreet, *Influencing Human Behavior* (New York: Norton, 1925), p. 82.

est and intensity. In order to achieve such crescendo, the sermon must include conflict and suspense. The element of surprise must be part of your sermon. Jay Adams says, "Cultivate in your sermons what is called 'the surprise power.' Don't say what people expect you to say. Let your thunderbolt drop out of a clear sky."[8]

Let there be a clash of forces throughout the message. In a good play there will be a conflict between personalities. The outcome should remain in doubt until the conflict is resolved. The preacher can do the same in terms of the crucial issues of life and the answers people give to these issues. Depict persons who have lived on both sides of the issues raised. That is easily done in a biographical sermon. The same technique may be used by introducing biblical or modern personalities into the various themes of your message.

A good play reaches the climax, then closes quickly. The same should be true of a sermon. All of us have experienced preaching past the best stopping point in our sermon. When that happens there is always a definite "let down" on the part of the people. When you reach your climax, bring your sermon to a graceful but quick close. Failure to do this will lessen the force and total impression of your message. You may actually undo what you had achieved earlier in your sermon.

Mark Twain illustrates my meaning: "When the speaker had talked ten minutes I was so impressed I decided I would give every cent I had with me. After another ten minutes I concluded that I would throw into the treasury all the silver I had about me. Ten minutes later I decided I wouldn't give anything, and at the end of the talk, still ten minutes later, as the contribution plate came around, I was so utterly exhausted by the arguments that I extracted two dollars for my own use."[9] Wrap up in a few brief, summary sentences the essence of what you are saying in your message. Leave the message with your hearers. Call for a decision.

8. Jay Adams, *Pulpit Speech* (Phillipsburg, N.J.: Presbyterian and Reformed, 1971), p. 36.
9. In Jones, p. 61.

Make the Bible Come Alive

Using dramatic techniques can help the Bible come alive as you preach. The Bible is not a dead book although too often we who preach God's Word make it appear that way. You can make Bible characters come alive through imaginative dialogue. Allow the Bible characters to speak. If you are preaching on the three Hebrew children in the fiery furnace, don't just recount the facts of the Bible narrative. Put the three young Hebrew men in the flames. Put words in their mouths. Let them speak in the language of today.

Storytelling

This brings us to the technique of storytelling. The effect of your sermon can be greatly enhanced through an understanding of how to use story material. Stories must be so told as to induce the feeling of reality by those who listen. To do this the artist uses illusion. The artist does not paint every tiny detail of a tree or flower. Rather, he leaves enough detail missing so that the viewer can fill in the details for himself. The preacher must do the same as he uses story material. We grow impatient with the person who gives us too many details. We want to use some imagination ourselves.

Preachers must learn the art of selection. Certain items must be included, but others must be excluded if we are to be effective in telling stories. When drawing a picture of a character, use only enough description to activate the listener's imagination. All details that are not essential should be eliminated. Describe the personalities in your story in such a manner that your listeners can see them. Use dialogue freely. That will make elaborate explanation unnecessary.

In telling a story for illustrative purposes the preacher will want to make use of slanting. You are perhaps familiar with the use of slanting in news reporting. Such slanting is not considered justifiable when the purpose of the report is to be objective, although it is considered perfectly acceptable in an editorial. A sermon is more like an editorial than a report of a fire or a robbery. We are not pretending to be objective in it. To the contrary, we are preaching for a verdict, and it is even necessary that we use slanted language in our descriptions of the characters in our illustrations so that they will come alive for our readers.

In storytelling, several principles of drama are vital. The beginning of the story must arouse interest and lead directly into the essentials of the story. The body of the story must have orderly development and constant movement. The element of suspense must be safeguarded. When a good story fails to "go over" it is often because the suspense has been lost. Do not give away your punch line.

As you learn to use dramatic techniques in your preaching, you will observe a greater interest on the part of your people. Through the years of my own study and practice in sermon delivery I have come to the conclusion that the preacher is chiefly responsible for the interest or lack of interest on the part of his listeners. We have a message that is eminently worthy of being heard and received. We must so present our message that it will be interesting and appealing to those who hear us. Some would say our job is not to make the gospel appealing; it is our job to make it available. I do not feel we are faced with that alternative. Rather, we are called to greater effectiveness in our delivery, so that we can make the gospel appealing as we make it available.

Henry Ward Beecher was dubbed the high priest of emotionalism by the literary historian Vernon L. Parrington. His sermons were so interesting that he filled Plymouth Congregational Church two times each Sunday for over forty years. Parrington describes Beecher this way: "Here he had room to display his dramatic talent when he stood to preach. Mimicking, thundering, imploring, berating, he would make his audiences laugh and cry. Frequently he would weep himself. He had a wide assortment of anecdotes, and used grotesque facial contortions to act out dialogues and pantomines. Once, pretending to be catching a trout, he cast an imaginary fly, hooked an imaginary fish, dodged up and down as he reeled in, and finally landed his quarry. It was all so vivid that a man in the front row stood up and shouted, 'my Lord, he's got him!' "

PART 4

Psychological Aspects of Sermon Delivery

I preached for years before I had any understanding of the psychological dynamics of the speaking situation. Yet to a large degree the whole matter of effective speaking is essentially psychological. Much of the training for public speaking today seems to miss that point altogether. It is certainly true of training in sermon delivery. Emphasis is placed upon the arrangement of ideas, sentence structure, enunciation and diction, gestures, and so on. Of course, all those matters are important. The preacher may be aware of them, and even use them effectively, and still be a failure in the pulpit. For this reason many preachers are wooden and unconvincing in their delivery.

The purpose of this section is to make you aware of the psychological dynamics involved in the delivery of a sermon. First is a discussion of modern communication. The communications revolution, especially the impact of television, has radically changed the preacher's task. He must be a better communicator than he has ever been before. Although I will discuss some of the problems created by the communications revolution, I will also point to some of the benefits that may be derived from it and, in addition, discuss the use of the technology that modern communications places in the hands of the preacher.

You will find the chapter on the preacher-audience dynamic interesting. Such matters as eye contact and getting and keeping attention will be discussed, along with practical hints to help you make the preacher-audience relationship an effective one. There is also a discussion on humor.

The last chapter of this section will deal with nonverbal communication. Body communication, including the use and abuse of gesture, is an important part of sermon delivery.

This entire section is designed to make you aware of the psychological dynamics involved in the preaching situation.

12

Sermon Delivery as Communication

In his book *Power in Expository Preaching* Whitsell says: "The supreme test of a sermon is whether or not it communicates."[1]

If the preacher is to be effective in sharing the Word of God with his people he must be vitally interested in communication. He must never allow his sermons to become polished works of sermonic art that cause people to praise him for his gifts of sermonic preparation. Neither must he allow his sermon to exist only for himself. The preacher must ensure that communication between the pulpit and the pew is always maintained.

Communications Revolution

Our generation is witnessing a communications revolution. A relatively new field of study, cybernetics, is the study of the mechanisms of communication, both human and electronic. The communications revolution has to do with the dramatic changes taking place in the field of communication as a result of the development of an almost infinite variety of technical electronic equipment.[2] Preachers who want to be heard must give careful attention to what is being done in modern communications. The secular world is serious about communication. Preachers can be

---

1. Farris D. Whitsell, *Power in Expository Preaching* (Old Tappan, N.J.: Revell, 1963), p. 133.
2. John R. W. Stott, *Between Two Worlds* (Grand Rapids: Eerdmans, 1982), p. 64.

no less serious. Those of us who stand before congregations week after week must be sure that we connect.

In one sense of the word, modern communications has brought a variety of competitors for the preacher. To be sure, preaching has always had its competition. In a previous day the dramatist, the newspaper writer, the author, and the playwright all competed for the ear of the people. The communications revolution has added other significant competitors. Today, the preacher competes with the television writer and producer. The people's ears are bombarded by the voices of the evening newscasters and the insistent appeals of contemporary musicians. By means of the most sophisticated technology, rival voices call the preacher's people to listen and to heed their appeals. Foolish is the preacher who fails to be aware of his competition.

Television

No technological advance has had as great an impact upon our society as has television. None of us would doubt that television is a major factor in our lives. Paul Lee Tan, in *Signs of the Times*, shares some enlightening information about television's impact upon our generation. He notes that "the A. C. Nielson company, which measures TV audiences and their behaviors, [has] revealed that in the average American home the TV is on six hours and fourteen minutes a day. This study, done in 1979, shows that this is two hours per day more than the daily average in 1969."[3] We are not yet aware of all the ramifications of such extended television viewing.

Television brings many benefits. People are more knowledgeable about a wider variety of events and experiences than previous generations have been. By means of public and network television they can attend great occasions. By means of cable television they can view films, plays, and political functions that otherwise would not be broadcast.

This wide exposure to ideas and events undoubtedly has an effect upon the preacher's assignment. Television makes it more

3. Rockville, Maryland: Assurance, p. 1439.

difficult for people to listen attentively to sermons. As a result, the preacher has a harder time gaining and holding the attention of his people. Newscasters are attractive and fluent in delivery. The advantages of teleprompters, on-the-spot reporters, and guest speakers are not feasible for the preacher. People listen to polished presentations on television. Then they come to church to listen to their preacher. He faces a more selective audience than did previous generations of preachers.

In addition, there are several negative tendencies of television. John R. W. Stott lists five of them. First, he points out that television has a tendency to make people physically lazy. Every conceivable entertainment is to be found within the comfort of one's den. Even a worship service is available. Why bother to get in a car, battle traffic, and sit in a crowded building to hear a sermon? Without question, television worship services provide an opportunity for the sick and elderly to hear the gospel. In some parts of the country where there is no clear-cut Bible witness, television makes it possible for people to hear the truth. On the other hand, worship by television does not provide fellowship or corporate witness.

Second, Stott says that though it is not always the case, television has a tendency to make people uncritical intellectually. With the increase in the number of channels available to the average viewer, programs with good intellectual content are more accessible than previously. People do have a tendency, however, to turn to television merely as a relaxer and entertainer. Then they tend to view, not analyze, what they see and hear there.

Third, television brings about emotional insensitivity. Upon first viewing, the horrors of war, the miseries of poverty, and the brutality of murder produce shock and concern. Viewed over a long period of time, however, the emotions of the viewers are likely to become jaded. The human personality can endure only a certain amount of pain and tragedy. There comes a time when the individual is left with little or no feeling.

Fourth, television creates psychological confusion. Much of the viewing matter on television deals with the artificial and contrived. The families portrayed are not real. The experiences through which they go may seem lifelike, but the viewer is aware as he watches the screen that the events depicted on the screen are not actually happening. Can people exposed constantly to unreality relate positively to the reality of the truth as it is revealed in Scriptures? Is the difficulty of moving from the world of fantasy to the real world too much to expect of people?

Stott finally says that television creates moral disorder in people. It has a subtle and damaging influence. Even sexual promiscuity and physical violence are frequently portrayed in television drama as normal. The impression is given that everybody does it. Godlessness and immorality are "in." Faith in God and old fashioned moral standards are "out."[4] Especially is this negative aspect of television damaging to children. Whereas American adults view television 23.3 hours weekly, surveys reveal that children of preschool age are the largest audience in America. Their weekly average viewing time is 30.4 hours.

Preachers must come to grips with the fact that their congregations have actually been brainwashed by television. We must not assume that people are anxious to hear what we have to say. We cannot be satisfied with average or below average presentations of our sermons. We are no longer allowed to be shabby in our presentation. If we do not "get with it," people will turn us off by the hundreds. A generation used to the swift-moving images of the television screen will not tolerate a boring, lifeless, drab presentation of the gospel. Our day of modern communications challenges us to deliver our sermons in the most attractive manner possible. By means of correct vocal techniques, color, and rhetorically effective delivery, we must preach the gospel to our generation.

Are you depressed? You need not be. Rather than being discouraged and defeated by the tremendous difficulties presented by our modern age of communication, I am greatly encouraged. First, I know that as a preacher of the gospel I have a miracle of communication at my disposal. I know that I do not have to communicate the Word of God merely using my own skills as a communicator. The indwelling Holy Spirit is able to take the

---

4. Stott, pp. 70-73.

sermon I preach and apply it with power and effectiveness to the minds and hearts of my listeners. Also, the modern communications revolution has placed in my hands wonderful tools to assist me in preaching the Word of God.

Communications Theory

Communications theory explains how the process of communication takes place. Four factors are involved in the communicative process. First is a source. This is the person who desires to communicate with others. Second is the message: what he desires to communicate. Third is the channel, or medium, in this case words. Fourth is the receiver, the object of the communication. The receiver must decode or interpret the message given.

One can easily see how these four factors apply to sermon delivery. The preacher is the source. He stands before a congregation, called of God to preach and gifted and empowered to do so. The message he takes from the Bible, places in his words, and conveys to the waiting congregation. The medium he uses is the spoken word. The receivers are the persons in the congregation. The listeners receive the words delivered by the preacher and then decode them in categories that are understandable to them.

In addition to the listeners' inner responses there will be overt responses as well. In the average congregation those reactions may not be readily apparent, but they are there just the same. The listeners may smile, laugh, wriggle, or yawn. Those little clues let the preacher know whether he is being understood or not. They also let him know if his message is being received favorably or unfavorably. At this point the preacher is not merely a transmitter but is also a receiver. Similarly, the listeners are not merely receivers but are transmitters too. You might think of a preacher, then, as a kind of "transceiver." As the preacher delivers his sermon he is at the same time responding to the feedback from his audience.

A final ingredient must be added to the preaching situation. Because a congregation has more than one listener, there is audience interstimulation and response. People laugh louder in a group because of the laughter of others. The mere presence of others directs the behavior of the individual.

Keeping these aspects of communication theory in mind will assist the preacher greatly. Much more is involved in being an effective speaker than one might assume. The preacher will be helped if he takes the attitude that he and his listeners are participating in the preaching situation as a group. His attitude is not one of "they, the audience and I, the speaker." Rather, his attitude is "you and I." The preacher must help his listeners sense that they are as much a part of the communicative process as is he. The idea is to create the feeling that "we are all thinking this through together." The more the preacher makes his listeners aware of their participation in what he is saying, the better he will communicate.[5]

The Motivational Cycle

Study in communications theory will also help the preacher understand how his listeners are motivated. Those in the field of speech communication talk about the motivational cycle. Five factors are involved.

First is the matter of *attention*. The average congregation will be attentive for only four minutes at a time. Therefore, the preacher must use many different devices to revive the attention of his listeners. He may employ the vocal variables. Pause can sometimes be an effective way to gain attention. Variety in volume can regain or lengthen attention. Throwing in a funny story can pick up attention. Using a change of voice in creative dialogue can do it.

The second factor in motivation is *need*. The preacher must establish early in his message some need his sermon can meet. This need must be universal, related to all people, and timeless. Let the preacher study the psychology of the human personality. The basic needs of men have not changed. The preacher will do well to study them.

Third is the factor of *satisfaction*. The preacher must show in his sermon how the need can be met. He can do that by apply-

5. Milton Dickens, *Speech: Dynamic Communication* (New York: Harcourt Brace Jovanovich, 1954), pp. 11-16.

ing the truths of the gospel to the contemporary needs of men.

Fourth is the factor of *visualization*. At this point the preacher brings his audience in for the first time. He has their attention. He has brought before them some particular need. He shows them how the need can be met. Now he enables the people to visualize how this need can be met in their own lives.

Fifth is the factor of *action*. At this point the preacher shows the people what the sermon calls them to do. This course of action will constantly be kept before the people throughout the message. Actually, the preacher begins his invitation in his introduction. Very early in the sermon he establishes the fact that they will be called upon to take a certain course of action.

Benefits of Modern Communication

Understanding and applying modern communications theory enables today's preacher to be both a man of the Word and a man who knows his world. There is every reason for the preacher to be knowledgeable about the world around him as he stands in the pulpit to preach. Your delivery will be more appealing as you learn through modern communications to apply your message to the modern conditions of life. By means of newspapers, magazines, and television your store of the knowledge of life as your people are experiencing it will be full. Also, we are learning that there is great appeal when the personal note is included in our presentations. Notice how the attempt is made in virtually every area of modern communications to touch people in a personal way. The television commercial admonishes us to "reach out and touch someone." The wise preacher will pick up on the need evident today for the one-on-one style of communication. Communication that meets needs is effective. The preacher who comes to his people with a solid Bible message must relate that message to the needs of his contemporary audience.

The advent of well-trained, skillful communicators in our society makes it almost mandatory that today's preacher preach without notes. Those who watch the skillful presentations of news people and entertainers will not be reached by the preacher who must be constantly looking down at his sermon outline or text. Any preacher with a genuine desire to share the message of God with others can learn to deliver a sermon with a minimum of material before him. In the next chapter I will discuss preacher-audience dynamics. By way of anticipation, eye contact cannot be what it is intended to be if the preacher is too dependent upon his notes.

Wise is the preacher who will take advantage of the technology the communications explosion has placed at his disposal. Very soon preachers will have computer programs available to enable them to do mountains of research in mere seconds. Such technology will greatly assist them in gathering material for their sermons. Also, preachers will be able to plug in to the great libraries of the nation. Knowledge will be at our fingertips as it has never been before. What a day to be a preacher!

Sound Reinforcement

Modern technology makes it possible for the preacher to have better sound reinforcement than any previous generation. Superior sound systems for church auditoriums are now available. Yet often that technology is not used in the churches. Our modern congregations go to the great entertainment centers of our nation. They hear superior sound. Then they go to church and try to listen to a preacher who labors before a microphone preserved from the 1930s. Speakers that seem to have come from a 1950s movie house bring the sound poorly to their ears. No wonder some preachers are never able to communicate. More than one preacher has lost his congregation because they literally could not hear him. In the latter part of the twentieth century there is no excuse for churches to have inferior sound reinforcement.

Learn how to use sound effectively. Be thoroughly acquainted with the techniques required in speaking before a microphone. Use the microphone as a tool. Have monitor speakers that pour the sound back on you. That will give you a sense of "presence" as you speak. If you can hear yourself, it will relax you and enable you to say what you want to say in the most effective and forceful manner. Decisions need to be made about how you will use your sound system. Will you use a wireless microphone or the pulpit microphone? I prefer using the pulpit mike. The negative factor in a pulpit mike is that is restricts my ability to move somewhat, but on the positive side it enables me to "milk" the mike. I can move in when I want to be softer and more intimate; then I can move back when I want to use more volume.

Get acquainted with the sound engineer. The man who operates your amplification system can actually make or break you. Dr. Brodnitz, in a rather sarcastic attitude, says: "Apart from distortion which poor equipment produces we are at the mercy of the sound engineer. This modern Pygmalion can create voices, almost out of nothing, by the witchcraft of his panel. He can blow up conversational speech to the dimensions of the arena. He can emphasize the lower or higher frequencies of our voice and thereby change its character completely."[6] Brodnitz is correct. Learn to work closely with your sound engineer. He can help you be a better communicator.

Rather than allow the difficulties of communication in this generation overwhelm you, use them to help you communicate in a more effective manner. Can you imagine what the apostle Paul would have done with the technology available to twentieth-century preachers? Preacher, go for it!

6. Friedrich Brodnitz, *Keep Your Voice Healthy* (Springfield: Ill.: Thomas, 1973), pp. 69-70.

13

The Preacher-Audience Dynamic

Ultimately, the preacher delivers his sermon for the glory of God. Practically, he delivers his message for the sake of an audience. His purpose is to reach the people who listen to him. For this reason he must be keenly conscious of the dynamics involved in the speaking situation.

Many preachers seem to have no awareness that anybody is listening while they preach. They are so filled with their subject they seem to have forgotten its object. Because the preacher is focused upon his subject matter, the bond of communication between himself and the congregation is broken. Actually, the subject matter is not the vital aspect of the preaching situation, the audience is. Therefore, if he concentrates his attention on the audience and carefully adjusts to their responses, he can control to a large degree the preaching situation. He can condense, expand, or vary his message as he proceeds. The preacher must learn to do audience-centered preaching rather than subject-centered preaching.[1]

In terms of preparation the preacher must keep in mind that he is gathering his material for a specific audience. The pastor who stands many times weekly before his congregation rarely has the luxury of preparing a message entirely in terms of himself. His message must be prepared with a specific audience in mind. Therefore, he must use the available means of spanning the distance between himself and his listeners. He must carefully ana-

1. Robert White Kirkpatrick, *The Creative Delivery of Sermons* (Joplin, Mo.: Joplin College, 1944), p. 14

lyze the audience before he prepares and delivers the message so
that what he says will be appropriate for them.

The Electric Spark

There is something exciting about what takes place between
a man and his audience when genuine preaching occurs. He
gathers his material in the study. Then he sets it on fire in the
pulpit. When a man speaks who has been saved and called to
preach, whose soul is on fire with truth, who speaks to other men
face to face and eye to eye, there is an electricity that flashes
between him and his people. A beautiful teamwork occurs in the
preaching event. The preacher and his listeners lift each other up,
higher and higher, until they are borne as on chariots of fire to
another world. In such a dynamic situation there is power to
move men, to change character and destiny. No other medium
possesses such power.[2]

The electricity that flows between the preacher and his people is the distinguishing mark of many of the great Bible exposi-
tors. Although their content was superior and their voices
appealing, a great deal of their effectiveness was due to the personal electricity that flowed between them and their congregations. This spark between preacher and people must be present if
preaching is to accomplish its intended end. Because of this
dynamic, a sermon is not to be regarded as something that exists
upon paper. Nor is a sermon a series of facts presented in an
appealing or interesting manner. Preaching is a two-way street.

Preaching was never intended to be a monologue delivered
for its own sake. The brethren in the church who are black have
much to teach the rest of us about genuine heartfelt worship.
Their worship services are unashamedly emotional and expressive. True audience participation occurs in the service. The wor-
shipers actually talk back to the preacher. He knows how to pace
himself accordingly. There is two-way communication. The
response of the congregation provides the preacher with inspira-

---

2. George Henderson, *Lectures to Young Preachers* (Edinburgh: B. McCall Bar-
    bour, 1961), p. 95.

tion and stimulation. He soars to the heights as he delivers his sermon.

The sermon will be effective when the preacher delivers it to the hearts of the people. He must not preach over their heads in flowery oratory or beneath their feet in trite expressions. He must go to their hearts with true, personal application. To be effective we must not merely preach before the people; we must preach to them. As we look at the people one by one, our whole demeanor and expression must indicate to them we have a message for their personal benefit.

If no two-way communication occurs, what is the point of preaching? A poor woman left the service of a prestigious church in Scotland. A famous and scholarly preacher had preached. When she left the service someone asked if she enjoyed the sermon. Her response was affirmative. She was also asked: "Were you able to follow him?" To which she replied: "Far be it from me to presume to understand such a great man as that!"[3] The story is somewhat humorous, but mostly sad. If we fail to connect with our listeners, we fail.

Every preacher will be much more effective if he will learn to preach to his audience, not en masse, but one by one. He should be aware of his hearers and observe their response to the message while he is preaching it. To do this the preacher must love his people. Richard Cecil, an Anglican preacher in London, said, "To love to preach is one thing, to love those to whom we preach is quite another."[4]

Eye Contact

Several psychological aspects of the preacher-audience dynamic must be understood if the preacher is to communicate to the people effectively. One of these is the importance of eye contact. Look at your audience. That will make your delivery much more effective. Cicero says, "In delivery, next to the voice in

3. In D. Martyn Lloyd-Jones, *Preaching and Preachers* (Grand Rapids: Zondervan, 1971), p. 122.
4. In Loyd-Jones, p. 92.

effectiveness is the countenance; and this is ruled over by the eye."[5]

Many congregations sense that the preacher is not really looking at them. He seems to be looking only toward them. That is extremely detrimental. The impression is given that the speaker is distant, aloof, or uninterested. Avoiding the listener's eyes sends a message of extreme discomfort or lack of interest. The preacher's credibility is reduced. Look into the eyes of the various members of the congregation. Any part of your audience constantly ignored will feel less and less involved in the preaching event.

Stott says: "Look at your people face to face and eyeball to eyeball. Always talk to people. Never merely spray the building with words."[6] The use of good eye contact may be the most effective means of nonverbal communication.

Looking at them will enable the preacher to pick up the response of his congregation. He can tell if they understand what he is saying and may thus adjust his message. If they do not seem to understand, he can repeat, simplify, or illustrate. If they are not interested, he can use a variety of means to stir their interest. He may adapt his style and manner to the response of his listeners. The preacher must be constantly searching for signs of the hearers' reactions to his message and modify his delivery accordingly. By their facial expressions, blandness, or frowns he may determine what they are thinking.

A few people in your audience will have unusually expressive faces. You can easily read their reactions at a glance. Should their eyes not meet yours for a period of time, chances are the attention of your audience is straying. Take this signal to change the pace of your message before your crowd becomes noticeably restless. I have found it helpful to isolate certain people in the congregation to serve as barometers.

To look individuals in the eye benefits the section in which they are sitting. You do not have to look at each person in the

5. In John A. Broadus, *The Preparation and Delivery of Sermons* (New York: Harper, 1926), p. 351.
6. John R. W. Stott, *Between Two Worlds* (Grand Rapids: Eerdmans, 1982), p. 252.

section. The fact that you are looking at one gives the entire section a feeling you are looking at them. Also, it creates a sense of expectancy. If you look at one person in the section, you may look at others. Be careful to include every section of your building in your eye contact.

Simple eye contact also suggests an interest in others. This might be called eye touching. Eye touching says you value another person's independence, knowledge, and friendship.[7]

Of course, there are occasions when you will look away from your audience. You may be describing a falling building and therefore you look upward as a gesture to convey the effect of height. Maybe you are telling a story and you wish to dramatize someone who was downcast or discouraged. You would naturally look down. On these occasions regain eye contact as soon as possible.

Failure to have eye contact with your audience will bring at least two bad effects. First, the sermon will become less intelligible and more uncertain in its results. Second, an impersonal attitude will creep into your delivery. The element of personal interest and concern will evaporate.

Attention

Getting and keeping attention is another important aspect of the preacher-audience relationship. When an army sergeant bellows, "Tenhup!" the private snaps to attention, freezes in position, and listens for the next command. When the television announcer says, "May we have your attention please? This program is interrupted to bring you a special news bulletin," you sit up in your chair, lean forward a bit, forget matters at hand, and prepare to hear the bulletin. When the quarterback barks the signals, each player on the team becomes rapt in his attention.

The average attention span is approximately four minutes, a span that will vary from audience to audience and even from individual to individual. As a result, the preacher must be constantly thinking about how to maintain the interest of his

7. Perry W. Buffington, "Psychology of Eyes," *Sky* 13, no. 2 (February 1984):92-96.

audience. He wants the people to hear what he has to say and then to respond to those truths. If his audience is not attentive, his goals in speaking to them cannot be achieved. Elwood Kratsinger invented an electronic device called the wiggle meter. The device recorded and measured the physical movements of an audience. The amount of interest of the audience could thereby be gauged. The wiggle meter indicated that the average person listening to interesting material sits quietly. When bored, he moves, looks around the room, and fidgets. The meter revealed that the attention of the average person listening to a speaker fluctuates. His attention is AC rather than DC.[8] The good preacher must not only catch attention, he must also maintain it.

There are several hindrances to audience attention. Using abstract words that are difficult to understand will cause the attention of an audience to lag. In our chapter on the use of words we indicated that words having few syllables are easier for most people to understand. Hackneyed ideas and phrases have a tendency to lower the attention level. People soon tire of hearing the same things over and over again. Also, the preacher who is pedantic and too detailed will bore his audience and cause them not to be attentive. Such a preacher's ideas seem to stand still. They do not move forward. The preacher whose personality is colorless, whose voice is monotonous, and whose bodily actions are rigid will have a difficult time maintaining interest.

Several other factors affect the attention level of an audience. The significance of what is being said is important. The average person in a congregation is most interested when the sermon affects him. Self-preservation, power, reputation, sentiments, tastes, and affections are some basic motives of human behavior. The preacher should strive to relate what he is saying to the people in his congregation. If the people hear something that significantly affects them, they will be more likely to listen.

People are also attracted by the unique. The preacher's topic may deal with something that is not normally discussed in the pulpit. The uniqueness of his subject matter will attract atten-

---

8. Milton Dickens, *Speech: Dynamic Communication* (New York: Harcourt Brace Jovanovich, 1954), p. 229.

tion. Caution must be exercised in this area, however. Preaching on particular subjects merely for the sake of their uniqueness may be dangerous. There is the tendency to promise more than you can deliver. Several years ago there was special interest in the subject of the second coming of Jesus. Dramatic events in current affairs had caused a renewed interest in what the Bible says about that event. I started a Sunday night series through the book of Revelation. The building actually filled up and over-flowed. People were greatly interested in the prophetic Scriptures. The wise preacher will take advantage of such interest, but he will be careful not to unduly sensationalize his subject.

People are normally attentive when a problem is posed for them to solve. The preacher may present a problem in the intro-duction of his sermon. He will involve his congregation in his thinking and logical progress as he solves the problem, and thereby he keeps his people with him throughout the message.

Most people are attracted by a good fight. Conflict will often gain attention. Dr. Jack Hyles, pastor of First Baptist Church, Hammond, Indiana, is an effective pulpit communica-tor. I heard him say several years ago that the way to draw a crowd is to get against something. Get against chocolate bars. Tell all the detrimental effects of eating chocolate. Warn of the dire results on the complexion through prolonged use of choco-late! There is certainly an element of truth in what Dr. Hyles says. That does not mean that the preacher must be constantly attacking everything that moves. Rather, it means that there is value in bringing the element of conflict into your sermons. By the use of dramatic dialogue, pit one Bible antagonist against another. The element of conflict will help maintain the attention of your people.

Phrasing

The use of variety throughout your sermon delivery will help maintain attention. I like to think in terms of three *p*'s in the matter of variety. The first *p* is *phrasing*. We discussed this in the section on the mechanical aspects of sermon delivery. Effective speech must have distinction in its phrasing. The preacher whose sermons change lives will learn not only accuracy but power in his use of phrasing. Know how to group words together. Know how to give proper emphasis to the main words in your phrases. Avoid not only the one-tone voice but the one-tone mind. The one-tone approach makes all matters in your phrase of equal value. There are no emphases, no hurrying over unimportant details, no slowing up at more significant phrases. There is only a steady drone. Avoid also the string-of-beads mind. In this approach one fact is strung along after another with no observable relationship between them. Keep your audience aware of the important facts in each phrase as you speak. [9]

Pause

Pause is one of the most useful tools in securing attention. Spurgeon says, "Pull up short every now and then, and the passengers on your coach will wake up. The miller goes to sleep while the millwheels revolve, but if by some means or other the grinding ceases, the good man starts and cries, What now? On a sultry summer's day, if nothing will keep off the drowsy feeling, be very short, sing more than usual, or call on a brother or two to pray. Make a point of interjecting arousing parentheses of quietude. Speech is silver, but silence is golden when hearers are inattentive. Keep on, on, on, on, with the commonplace matter and monotonous tone, and you are rocking the cradle, and deeper slumbers will result; give the cradle a jerk, and the sleep will flee."[10] Well said, Spurgeon.

Change of Pace

The third way to use variety is the change of pace. You must change pace or you will lose the attention of your audience. The object of this method is to keep your audience rested, refreshed, and

9. H. A. Overstreet, *Influencing Human Behavior* (New York: Norton, 1925), pp. 83-84.
10. Charles H. Spurgeon, *Lectures to My Students* (London: Marshall, Morgan and Scott, 1954), p. 138.

anxious to go on with you. Change of pace may be changed in any number of ways. You may do so by a quick change in speech content. Tell a story, a joke, or make a pointed remark. Just be sure your story or whatever is related to the last thing you said before your change of pace. The preacher may direct a remark to some well-known individual in his audience. This never fails to arouse a lethargic audience, especially the dear brother you address! Change of pace may also be achieved by lowering the voice in volume, pitch, or both. Do something to change pace. Pause, cough, tell a funny story, slap on the podium, raise your voice, whisper—do something. I once heard W. A. Criswell stop in the middle of a sermon and give three cheers for the Baylor football team! I assure you he had the attention of the people again.

Humor

Humor is one of the preacher's greatest assets. Used in proportion and properly, humor can be invaluable to the preacher. The proper use of humor involves the audience, produces lively bodily reactions, and maintains a sense of proportion in the message. Of course, humor can be used too much and abused. I am thinking not so much of joke-telling as I am of an attitude of playfulness, an attitude of not taking oneself too seriously—the ability to suddenly twist a word, or to present the grotesque idea. The humorous person causes us to respond immediately to him. He makes us comfortable. Furthermore, he is not completely predictable. We never know what he might say. He may say just the opposite of what the situation calls for. The humorous person is playful, creative, and not afraid of laughing at himself. In other words, he is everlastingly and refreshingly unexpected.

Another benefit in the use of humor in a sermon is that it often breaks the tension of the moment. People cannot maintain attention for a long period of time. Neither can they endure highly emotional material indefinitely. They need to come back down and relax for a few moments. Humor can do that. Also, it can tear down the barriers people are prone to erect between themselves and the preacher. If you can get your audience to laugh, they are more likely to be receptive to what you have to say.

There are several kinds of humor: exaggeration, deliberate understatement, sudden change of thought, surprise thoughts, afterthoughts, the twisting of ideas, misinterpretation of the facts, intentional errors, restatement of a well-known quotation to give it a humorous twist, pantomime, poorly timed gestures, facial grimaces, anecdotes, impersonation of a character, and clever wording.[11]

Avoid using canned humor. Ready-made jokes normally fall flat. Use humor only if you can do so naturally. If it is not natural to you, then do not use it. Most of us do have a humorous side to our personality. It should be developed.

Let me make several suggestions concerning the way you use humor. Do not announce your efforts at humor. Let them come naturally. To signal the impression you are striving at humor will normally ensure that you are not humorous. Watch the response of your audience and adapt to it. Sometimes, your remark after their response can be funnier than what you said at first. Always have a purpose in humor. Never use humor for its own sake. Instead, use it to make or emphasize a point. If you are going to take advantage of anyone in your humor, be sure it is yourself. Learn to time the punchline. Too many preachers run past the punchline, and the people miss the joke altogether.

The secret of the preacher's success in communicating to his audience has been succinctly summarized: "Hook them, hold them, hang on to them, humor them, and hit them."[12] That statement summarizes what I am trying to say about holding the attention of your audience.

We must always be aware that we are preaching before people. The intensity of what we say and our desire to say it must be obvious. There must be such fervor and fire in our message that the people cannot get away from it. There must be such a holy urgency about what we say that we take the attention of the people by storm. We should so speak that the people find they must listen. We can better do this when we understand and skillfully use the dynamics of the preacher-audience relationship.

---

11. Josh McDowell, "Syllabus on Communication and Persuasion" (© Josh McDowell, 1983. Mimeographed), p. 18.
12. Stott, p. 248.

14

Communicating
with the Body

The story is told of trouble between a preacher and his choir. The situation had become so serious that although the choir solemnly filed into the choir loft, when the time for singing came, they were as mute as oysters. The pastor, instantly sensing their motive, stood up and announced the hymn: "Let those refuse to sing who never knew our God"—with a pronounced gesture toward the choir loft. Then, facing the audience, with a sweep of his arms he proclaimed, "But children of the heavenly king may speak their joys abroad!"

Some thoughts are better expressed by gesture than by words. Fingers on closed lips are sometimes more effective than saying: "Don't speak." Outstretched arms mean more to a little child than merely saying, "Come here." Pointing the finger to the door often more effectively says, "Leave the room," than any language could express it.

Kinesics

Gesture is part of what is known as nonverbal communication. When you preach to your congregation you convey your message in two ways. You speak by means of words—verbal communication. You also speak by means of body language—nonverbal communication. Those two means of communicating must complement and support one another. Should they conflict, the nonverbal message is more likely to be believed than the verbal one.

Nonverbal communication has been given increased attention from communication experts in recent years. Their research has shown that nonverbal signs and symbols are much more significant than was previously imagined. The term *kinesics* has to do with the interaction between what the voice is saying and what the body is saying. Normally the relationship is called body language. Studies have revealed that 7 percent of the impact of a speaker's message comes through his words; 38 percent springs from his voice; whereas 55 percent comes from facial expressions.[1]

Those facts have importance for the preacher. Effective delivery must include a conscious and appropriate use of nonverbal communication. The preacher soon discovers that he is still communicating even when he is not speaking. Feelings are communicated nonverbally. Facial expression, eye contact, body tension, and tone of voice give your listeners clues as to what you really feel about God, yourself, and them. If the preacher's voice lacks feeling and his body is not responsive to what he says, he is not likely to be heard.

The preacher should use his whole body as he preaches. Bodily action is twofold: First, there is overt action, the movements of the body that are clearly observable. Overt action involves the conspicuous play of the muscles and major members of the body. Second, there is covert action, the action that involves subtle muscle tensions and relaxations.[2] The body is an active participant in effective sermon delivery. There must be body projection while the preacher preaches. Such body involvement is sometimes referred to as presence, and it is very important. The whole body is brought into play to some extent in all gestures, for gestures are themselves preceded by subtle or more obvious muscle tensions.

The countenance of the preacher also is vital in good pulpit communication. Cicero said that the countenance is next to the voice in importance in effective delivery. He further stated that

1. Haddon W. Robinson, *Biblical Preaching* (Grand Rapids: Baker, 1980), p. 193.
2. Anna Lloyd Neal, *A Syllabus for Fundamentals of Speech* (Greenville, S.C.: Bob Jones U., 1977), p. 46.

the countenance is ruled by the eyes.[3] In the previous chapter we discussed the importance of good eye contact. The eyes are the most eloquent part of the body. They have such expressive power that they control to some extent the expression of the whole countenance. By them we search and discover. By them we project cheer, fear, or anticipation. Who has not been enchanted by the dancing eyes of a little child or depressed by the empty stare of the terminally ill?

Physiologists have estimated that the facial musculature is such that more than 20,000 different facial expressions are possible.[4] Television has called attention to the importance of facial expressions. An audience looks at the preacher as much as it listens to him. Therefore, you must be ready to communicate facially as well as vocally. A fleeting glance may speak volumes. A curl of your lip or a twitch of your nostrils can convey instantly your feelings to the audience.

Gestures

Then there is the matter of gesture. Some textbooks on speech and sermon delivery contain elaborate discussions of the subject, but for the most part those discussions are of little use to the preacher. One of the worst things a preacher can do is create an atmosphere of artificiality by means of gestures that are obviously practiced. I have seen preachers whose gestures are so preplanned that they actually take away from the message rather than add to it. There is a better way to understand and utilize the place of gesture in body communication.

Gesture is any movement that helps express or emphasize an idea or emotional response. In some ways gesture embraces the entire field of kinesics. Included are clearly discernible bodily movements and all subtle changes of posture and muscle tone.

Some think of gesture only in terms of overt actions of the hands or arms and perhaps of the head. This understanding is

3. In John A. Broadus, *The Preparation and Delivery of Sermons* (New York: Harper, 1926), p. 350.
4. Loren Reid, *Speaking Well* (New York: McGraw-Hill, 1977), p. 243.

limited in that the various parts of the body do not function separately. Rather, they involve a follow-through that both is affected by and affects the whole body's degree of muscle tension. Gesture cannot actually be considered apart from an awareness of the body as a whole. As the preacher learns to use his body in preaching, his muscles learn to respond without apparent prompting or effort. The essence of effective gesture lies in timing. Any gesture used in a message should accompany or precede the key word or phrase it describes.

Spurgeon has an interesting as well as humorous discussion of the problems of gesture. He talks about the stiff gesture. He says: "Men who exhibit this horror appear to have no bend in their bodies and to be rigid about the joints. The arms and legs are moved as if they were upon iron hinges and were made of exceedingly hard metal. A wooden anatomical doll, such as artists use, might well represent their limbs so straight and stiff, but it would fail to show the jerks with which those limbs are thrown up and down."

Next he mentions the regular mechanical gesture. He describes those gestures as used by men who seem not to be living beings possessed of will and intellect. They appear to be mere automatons formed to go through prescribed movements at precise intervals.

He also talks about the ill-timed gesture. In this example he refers to the preacher whose hands do not keep time with his lips. He says: "The good brother is a little behind hand in his action, and therefore the whole operation is out of order. You cannot at first make the man out at all; he appears to chop and thump without rhyme or reason, but at last you perceive that his present action is quite appropriate to what he said a few seconds before."[5]

For gestures to be effective they must be appropriate. You should suit the action to the word and the word to the action. In a sense, the preacher gives two speeches at the same time: that which his listeners hear and that which they see. To be the most

---

5. Charles H. Spurgeon, *Lectures to My Students* (London: Marshall, Morgan and Scott, 1954), pp. 289-95.

effective, the preacher should mold the two speeches to form one communicative process.

I do not take the view that gesture should be practiced. In earlier years speakers were trained in elocution and expression, with extensive study given to gesture. Today, such training is considered unnecessary at best and harmful to good communication at worst. Hand and arm movements as a separate part of speech training is of little concern to the preacher. What the preacher does need to know is that gesture is a definite part of bodily action and should naturally result from an intelligent response to the content of his sermon. If a movement of the hand does not assist in communicating the sermon, it is not gesture. It is only a distracting and annoying movement that calls attention to itself. My conviction is that natural impulse should be the foundation of all gesture.

Make Gestures Your Servants

Gesture is genuine and true only when it is spontaneous and actually unconscious. Make gestures the servants of your thoughts and feelings. Let them arise naturally from what you are saying. If you are talking about a church steeple, the mental pictures behind your words should affect your gesture as well. When I see a steeple I naturally want to raise my hands and lift my eyes as if to point to the steeple. When I talk about the world I not only see the world, but with my hands and arms I form the world. What I am saying is, let your gestures be consistent with the meaning of what you say. A preacher should not be the product of a marriage between a phonograph and a windmill. Nor should he be, to misuse Shakespeare, "full of sound and fury, signifying nothing."[6]

My perception is that bodily movement, facial expression, and gesture are in much the same position as the variables in our vocal mechanism. When we see the words we are saying and feel the emotions that flow from our words, correct bodily actions

6. Robert King, *Forms of Public Address* (Indianapolis: Bobbs-Merrill, 1969), p. 2. The quotation is from *Macbeth*, act 5, sc. 5., lines 27-28.

will naturally occur without our giving conscious attention to them.

Body communication that is consistent with the words we say can be extremely effective. That is true as well of facial expression. If our facial expressions are consistent with our message, the people will understand we are sincere. Nonverbal expressions such as frowns, excitement, concern, smiles, or happiness help the listener sense that we are truly involved in what we are saying. The preacher who stands before his listeners stiff and rigid creates extreme discomfort in his audience and raises questions about his confidence and sincerity. On the other hand, the preacher who is alive to his message will communicate more effectively with his listeners. Effective body communication lends action to one's message. Demosthenes was a great public speaker. He said there are only three fundamentals of good speaking: action, action, and action. He was not merely equating action with emotion, nor was he talking about flamboyant gestures. He meant rather that the message had a force or enlivening power about it.[7] The same can be said of the good preacher.

A sermon is effectively delivered bodily when every action so definitely adds to the effectiveness of the ideas it expresses that the listeners are not consciously aware of the bodily movements at all. On a Sunday morning a sincere, earnest country preacher was preaching on his favorite subject—the story of David and Goliath. Rather dramatically he recounted how little David whirled the sling around his head and sent the smooth stone unerringly to Goliath's forehead. As the preacher came to the climax of his sermon his voice rose high with excitement: "You see folks, the whole point is it wasn't just that little rock that kilt that big bloke—it was the way that kid throwed it!"[8] Effective sermon delivery is not merely speaking a sermon to your people. Be aware of how you "throw" it.

Spend some time preparing for sermon delivery by giving attention to its nonverbal aspects. Just as you would work on the different aspects of effective vocal delivery, you might give some

7. R. C. Forman, *Public Speaking Made Easy* (Grand Rapids: Baker, 1967), p. 61.
8. In Kenneth McFarland, *Eloquence in Public Speaking* (Englewood Cliffs, N.J.: Prentice-Hall, 1961), p. 152.

attention to effective body communication. I am not recommending that you practice specific gestures. Rather, I am suggesting that you might be aware of the responses your body makes as you think and speak your words in normal conversation. Notice how your eyes and the muscles in your face and body respond to what you are saying, even without apparent prompting or effort. Pay attention, as well, to what you do with your hands. All of your gestures, you will observe, come naturally as a result of what you are saying. Why should not the same be true during the delivery of a sermon?

Giving attention outside the pulpit to gestures, facial expressions, and eye movements may help you use them more naturally and effectively in the pulpit. Some preachers respond bodily to their material with greater ease than do others. If you have difficulty in using your body, practicing while reading aloud might help you. Large, exaggerated movements in practice will have a tendency to set your body free. Read a sermon aloud. Move freely about the room. Respond consciously with pronounced movements to the content of what you are reading. Such overt response will have a tendency to train your muscles to respond to what you say in the pulpit. As you practice, talk with your hands. Use any movements that help you communicate the content of what you are reading.

Practice in this manner will also help you catch any habitual bodily movements that are likely to distract your audience and actually hinder communication. We all have a tendency to develop repetitious movements—raising and lowering a hand, tilting the head—that direct attention to ourselves and keep the audience from fully concentrating on the sermon.

Effective, expressive gestures are beneficial in several ways. They greatly assist verbal communication. They help us explain and picture what we are saying. They help our audiences see birds soar, walls topple, and arrows fly.

Good bodily movement is a positive factor in holding attention. Motion pictures and television have geared our people to fast moving, rapid-paced action. The preacher who stands lifelessly and listlessly in the pulpit almost guarantees that his audience will be disinterested.

Good bodily involvement in our message will make those in our audience sense that they are truly a part of the sermon. As we react expressively to the subject matter, they will react. If we frown as we describe taking a dose of castor oil, they will too. They will be empathic to what we have to say. Get your audience to react as you do to the various ideas of your sermon. They will become creatively involved in your sermon.

Bodily movement should be original and varied. Just as sameness in vocal expression will tend toward boredom, so too will repetition of any movement or gesture. Our body is capable of an amazing number of gestures and movements. Use a wide variety of them as you preach.

Effective sermon delivery involves not only speaking the message with your voice but saying it with your body as well. Shakespeare said: "There was speech in their dumbness, language in their very gesture."[9] Let your body speak for you.

9. William G. Hoffman, *How to Make Better Speeches* (New York: Funk & Wagnalls, 1976), p. 102. The quotation is from *The Winter's Tale,* act 5, sc. 2, line 12.

PART 5

Spiritual Aspects of Sermon Delivery

I have not reserved my discussion of the spiritual aspects of sermon delivery for last because of their lack of importance. Actually, the opposite is true. I consider the spiritual aspects of sermon delivery to be the most crucial. The greatest need in the modern pulpit is a sincerity and earnestness of heart that can only be produced by the power of the Holy Spirit. If the preacher has the power of God upon him when he prepares and as he preaches, his sermon will communicate in a creative, powerful, and lasting manner. If the Spirit's anointing is lacking, none of the other aspects of delivery can make up for its absence.

In the Old Testament, extensive preparation was made for the designing and planning of the Tabernacle. Meticulous attention was given to every detail of its construction. Moses built the structure according to pattern. When completed, however, the Tabernacle was little more than an elaborate, expensive box. Only when the glory of the Lord came down and filled it did the Tabernacle vibrate with the very life of God. The same is true in the preparation and delivery of sermons.

The preacher may be properly trained. He may have college and seminary degrees. He may even have an earned doctorate. His sermon may be a masterpiece of homiletical genius. His delivery may be flawless. Every aspect of his vocal equipment may be correctly utilized. But without the blessing of the Holy Spirit upon what he says, the preacher's sermon will not be effective.

I have tried to write this section from the top of my head and the bottom of my heart. This section has two chapters that I consider to be of paramount importance in effective sermon delivery. The first of these chapters is a discussion of the nature of heart preaching—a brief description of the element of heart in sermon delivery that characterized great preaching in the past and an enumeration of the benefits of heart preaching. There is also a discussion of the ingredients necessary to make one a heart preacher.

The final chapter concerns anointed preaching. My purpose is to indicate the teaching of the Bible concerning the role of the Holy Spirit in sermon delivery. The advantages and blessings of anointed preaching both for the preacher and the people are discussed. Also, I give some indication of the means whereby the preacher may have the anointing of God upon him as he preaches.

This section is not academic with me. The matters discussed are deeply personal and make up an indispensible part of my own philosophy of and approach to sermon delivery. I earnestly ask you to read these chapters with an open and receptive heart. Apprehension of the truths contained in them and utilization of these truths can transform your preaching ministry.

15

Heart Preaching

There is a scarcity of heart preaching today. Few preachers seem to have the element of "heart" in their preaching styles. Yet a casual survey of the preachers in the Bible indicates that they preached not only from their heads but also from their hearts.

Heart Preachers

Jesus was a heart preacher. He became so moved He actually wept over those before whom He ministered. As He viewed Jerusalem He wept. When He spoke to the disciples on the Emmaus road, there was such earnestness and fervor about His words that they declared: "Did not our heart burn within us, while He talked with us by the way, and while He opened to us the scriptures?" (Luke 24:32). Their hearts burned because His did.

Paul was a heart preacher. One of the early church fathers said he wished he could have seen three things: Solomon's Temple in its glory; Rome in its prosperity; and Paul preaching. Listen to him express the deep conviction of his heart: "I say the truth in Christ, I lie not, my conscience also bearing me witness in the Holy Ghost, that . . . I could wish that myself were accursed from Christ for my brethren, my kinsmen according to the flesh" (Rom. 9:1-3). Those are not the words of cool logic. They are words from the furnace of the soul. Paul preached with heart.

Great preachers of the past preached with heart. John Knox, who prayed, "Give me Scotland or I die," was a man who preached with heart. When he was an old man, he had to be helped to the pulpit. But as he prayed for the lost of Scotland, strength was given him, and he almost shook the pulpit apart because of his burden for lost men. Hugh Latimer was a preacher of the English Reformation. Someone said of him: "He spoke from the heart and his words went to the heart."[1] This note of sincerity and depth of feeling has characterized the great preachers throughout the history of the Christian church.

Many of the preachers who have moved me in my own lifetime were heart preachers. I can still recall some of the dear men of God who stirred my soul and moved me to tears, though I was just a young person. They did not do this merely by telling emotional stories. I knew that what they were saying came from their hearts. They may not have been the most scholarly men who ever preached. Their delivery may not have measured up to the standards I have presented in this book. Nevertheless, there was something about them that gripped me and moved me as I listened.

In my own Southern Baptist denomination I have heard many of the great preachers. They were all men of pathos and heart-stirring appeal. Though I did not hear him in person, I have heard tapes of the great preacher George W. Truett. He still moves me through his taped messages. In addition to a remarkable eloquence, R. G. Lee demonstrated a remarkable earnestness in his preaching. I can still recall hearing him speak at Southern Baptist conventions. He would move the audience like leaves in a strong summer wind. W. A. Criswell, beloved pastor of First Baptist Church, Dallas, Texas, is a heart preacher. Never will I forget traveling almost one hundred miles one way for four nights to hear him preach. Each night he preached with unusual appeal. My life as a young preacher has been shaped by men who knew how to preach with heart.

We need a return to heart preaching. Perhaps some would use other terminology. Perhaps you would prefer the term sincerity. Or maybe you like the word earnestness. Whatever you choose to call it, we desperately need it!

---

1. In John R. W. Stott, *Between Two Worlds* (Grand Rapids: Eerdmans, 1982), p. 26.

Charles Spurgeon comments on this necessary ingredient in preaching:

> A blacksmith can do nothing when his fire is out, and in this respect he is the type of a minister. If all the lights in the outside world are quenched, the lamp which burns in the sanctuary ought still to remain undimmed; for that fire no curfew must ever be rung. We must regard the people as the wood and the sacrifice, well wetted a second and a third time by the cares of the week, upon which, like the prophet, we must pray down the fire from heaven. A dull minister creates a dull audience. You cannot expect the office-bearers and the members of the church to travel by steam if their own chosen pastor still drives the old broad wheeled waggon.[2]

Spurgeon is talking about heart preaching. When the preacher's heart is on fire, his speech comes as lava from a volcanic flow. We desperately need this element in modern preaching. Preaching, to be genuinely effective, must be eloquence on fire. The preacher must preach from his heart as well as from his head. He must combine proper exposition with heartfelt exhortation.

A Return to Tears

Modern preaching has become too dry-eyed. There needs to be a return to genuine, heartfelt weeping in the pulpit. Joel admonishes: "Let the priests, the ministers of the Lord, weep between the porch and the altar" (Joel 2:17). We have about lost our capacity to weep. We have become so professional, academic, and intellectual that we do not seem to feel what we say as we should. There even seems to be an aversion to any expression of emotion in the pulpit. This is not an affliction common to liberal preachers only. Conservatives suffer from the same malady. We are much too casual and matter-of-fact in our preaching. This kind of preaching will not move modern men. Samuel

---

2. Charles H. Spurgeon, *Lectures to My Students* (London: Marshall, Morgan and Scott, 1954), pp. 306-7.

May said to Lloyd Garrison: "Oh my friend, do try to be more cool; why, you are all on fire." Garrison replied: "I have need to be on fire, for I have mountains of ice about me to melt."

Sermons are actually born in the heart. Though the preacher gets his sermon from the Bible, he must bring it to life in his heart. Though he may prepare his sermon on paper, he must deliver it from his heart. A distinction must be made between the preparation of a sermon and the act of delivering the sermon. In one sense, the two are not the same. A man went to hear George Whitfield preach and asked if he might print his sermons. Whitfield replied: "Well, I have no inherent objection, if you like, but you will never be able to put on the printed page the lightning and the thunder."[3]

Only heart preaching will stir others to action. A sermon is not a sermon if there is no heartbeat. The preacher must not merely communicate the contents of a message to his audience; he must also communicate his own heartbeat. In addition, he must stir the heartbeats of his hearers so that they will act upon the truths he presents to them. Only heart preaching will move the hearts of people. The psalmist declares: "Deep calleth unto deep" (Ps. 42:7). Today's preachers have plenty of education. They are polished and proper. They know how to present the gospel perhaps better than any previous generation of preachers. But the element of heart must be added to their training if they are to be permanently and eternally effective. Congregations must not only be mentally stimulated by the sermon, they must be emotionally stabbed by it as well.

In this connection, the role of the people in the pew in the preaching dynamic must also be considered. There must be cooperation on the part of the listeners if the preacher is to preach with heart as much as he desires. Many years ago I heard someone say that the average congregation places its preacher in a refrigerator, then expects him to sweat. A cold, lifeless, indifferent congregation can greatly hinder the preacher who genuinely wants to communicate the message from his heart. But the

3. In D. Martyn Lloyd-Jones, *Preaching and Preachers* (Grand Rapids: Zondervan, 1971), p. 58.

preacher should not let lack of response in the pew hinder him from preaching with his heart. Who knows? A weekly diet of heart preaching may thaw out many a cold heart in the congregation. So many congregations have not heard heartfelt preaching in so long that they actually do not know how to respond to it.

Perhaps the reason there has been a recoil against heart preaching is the extreme to which some preachers have gone. There is an insincerity that is obnoxious in the pulpit, if not embarrassing. The preacher who sheds crocodile tears and who purposely works up his congregation to accomplish his own ends is not actually a heart preacher. Such preaching is basically insincerity covered with a pretense of emotion. This kind of insincerity should not cause us to abandon real earnestness and sincerity in our preaching.

We are witnessing a strange inconsistency at present. Ours is an emotion-centered generation. Contemporary young people are listening to music that actually assaults their emotions. The amusements of our time are designed to create innumerable thrills and chills. Young people are passing churches in droves on their way to other places to have their emotional needs met. Why should the preacher not present the genuine sources of emotional satisfaction? Why should the preacher present the ultimate answers to the problems confronting people today in such an unemotional, lackadaisical manner?

Heart Preaching Is Soul Preaching

In real preaching the preacher delivers his soul. When I was a boy I recall hearing preachers say at the conclusion of their sermons: "Beloved, I have delivered my soul to you this morning." I have come to understand that this is very true in the matter of preaching. The preacher not only delivers his sermon; he also delivers himself. The preacher actually gives himself to the Lord and to his congregation. By means of his voice, his gestures, his intellect, and his heart he lays before the throne of God and the hearts of the people his very life. In one sense of the word we might say that sermon delivery is not so much the art of the preacher's delivering a sermon as it is of the preacher's delivering himself. The genuinely effective preacher is one who puts everything he has into his sermon. When he speaks, his sincerity and enthusiasm generate sparks. That kind of effectiveness cannot be imitated, for sincerity and earnestness are impossible to manufacture. They come from deep within the heart and spirit of a preacher. The preacher expresses them in his own individual way.

Heart preaching is the secret of eloquence. William Jennings Bryan defined eloquence as "the speech of one who knows what he is talking about and means what he says. It is thought on fire."[4] God must create this eloquence in the heart of a man. Moses was not by nature a speaker. He was a timid, hesitant man. Moses became an eloquent man because God made him eloquent. God gave Moses a ministry to perform, a story to tell, a message to deliver. That is what made Moses eloquent. It will make you eloquent as well.

The preacher who learns to preach from his heart will move men to action. Our purpose is not merely to present a Bible message for the purpose of information or display. We preach in order to bring men to decision. Our purpose is to change behavior for the better, to bring men to obedience to God, and to lead them to accept the challenge of a Christ-centered life. Heart preaching will help us accomplish those goals. When Cicero spoke to the people it was said, "How well Cicero speaks." But when Demosthenes spoke the people said: "Let us march against Carthage."[5]

What Makes a Heart Preacher?

We desire to be heart preachers. What are the ingredients that make one this kind of preacher? Let me mention some of them. First, the preacher must have a genuine, personal, and intimate walk with God. His call to preach must be definite. He

---

4. In Kenneth McFarland, *Eloquence in Public Speaking* (Englewood Cliffs, N.J.: Prentice-Hall, 1961), p. 17.
5. Ibid., p. 29.

must know that God has placed the burden of the Word of the Lord upon him. He must maintain the reality of that call by a strong devotional life. As he spends time alone with God in Bible study and prayer, he must cultivate the reality of God in his life. Scientists may lose God in the laboratory. Let the preacher take care that he does not lose God in his study. The sacred truths he handles weekly must not become unfelt truths to him. On his knees before the Lord his sermons will take possession of his heart. Their substance will become real in his own experience. He will preach his sermon to himself in the presence of the Lord. Then, when he stands to preach, his message will not come merely from his notes or from his mind, but from the depths of his heart.

Another essential ingredient of a heart preacher is love for people. Though the preacher must never fear men, he must desperately love them. Stott says, "It has to be admitted that some preachers enjoy thundering forth God's judgements. They find a morbid satisfaction in seeing their audience writhe under the lash of their whip."[6] He further adds: "Sometimes preachers use the pulpit to preach Good Chidings rather than Good Tidings."[7] Ask God to give you a love for the people before whom you stand to preach. One of the best ways to learn to love people is to be a personal soul winner. Preachers have become so much like business executives they have little time for personal work. Weekly going into the homes of lost people and presenting the gospel will help the preacher keep a warm, loving heart. If people know you love them and are genuinely concerned for their souls, you may say most anything you want to say.

I remember well the preacher who led me to Christ. He was not a great preacher. He was never asked to speak on conference programs. To my knowledge, his sermons were never published. But when I was only a nine-year-old boy, the reflection of the church lights upon the tears that coursed down his cheeks made an indelible impression upon my young heart. He loved people. He loved me. He did not reach me with his head. He reached me with his heart. John Newton said his preaching was to break a

6. Stott, p. 212.
7. Ibid.

hard heart and to heal a broken heart.[8]

Heart preaching results when the preacher is gripped by certain convictions. He is moved by the truths of God's Word. To be unmoved by the great truths of the Bible indicates one has never really understood what they mean. Man has a heart as well as a head. Who can be unmoved by the truth that God loves us, though we have desperately sinned against him? Who can remain untouched in his heart by the truth that Jesus Christ loved us so much He was willing to suffer at Calvary an infinite burden of sin in a finite period of time? It is unthinkable that the preacher who believes and preaches these truths should be dull or boring. Rather, the most exciting, the most thrilling, the most gripping subjects in the universe are dealt with by the faithful Bible preacher. For if he himself has been gripped by these truths he cannot help but stir those who hear him speak. We cannot be like the boring preacher mentioned by Martyn Lloyd-Jones. Lloyd-Jones said of him: "The good man was talking about fire as if he were sitting on an iceberg."[9]

Can we talk about the lostness of men and not be stirred in our hearts? Can we look into hell with no emotion? The truths of the Bible are not dead. They are living. The Bible is not a museum piece to be indifferently held up before people. Rather, the Bible is God's living Word to living men. God is speaking to men today through His Word. Proper comprehension and appreciation of Bible truths will make a man a heart preacher.

No preacher really becomes a heart preacher until he has experienced heartbreak himself. Throughout the Scriptures, God has a way of bringing blessing out of brokenness. The broken flask produced the fragrant odor (Mark 14:3). Jesus broke the loaves of bread and blessed them (Mark 8:6). God seems to use nothing until it is broken. Many great preachers have experienced their personal Gethsemane; then they became heart preachers. George W. Truett experienced the heartbreak of accidently killing a close friend in a hunting accident. Through personal agony and heartbreak God made Truett a heart preacher.

8. Ibid., p. 314.
9. Lloyd-Jones, p. 88.

G. Campbell Morgan heard a gifted young preacher. He commented to his wife that the young man was a very good preacher. His wife responded: "Yes, and he will be a better preacher when he has suffered some." This has been true in my own experience. Through a personal sorrow in my own family God taught me the lessons of a broken heart. A handicapped child has taught me many lessons in the school of brokenness. Whatever evidence of heart preaching may be found in my own ministry I attribute to a deeper personal experience with God through a trying time of heartbreak. When our hearts are broken, we learn how to preach to others who have broken hearts. Preaching is to break hard hearts and heal broken hearts. That is most effectively done when the preacher has been through his own valley.

When the preacher learns to preach from his heart he will preach with sincerity and earnestness. That will ensure that he has a genuine desire to share with his people. Every aspect of sermon delivery will benefit when the preacher preaches from his heart. Stay with God until He makes you a heart preacher. Learn that sermons are not delivered after a week of study. Nor are they delivered effectively simply by reading a book on the techniques of sermon delivery. They are delivered out of a life of heart preparation. In every congregation there are people with heavy hearts. They need to hear preaching that will reach their hearts.

George W. McDaniel, pastor of First Baptist Church, Richmond, Virginia, in the early years of the twentieth century, tells this story. At the time a singer named Frank W. Cunningham was known as Richmond's "sweet singer." A few years before Mr. Cunningham died he took Pastor McDaniel with him to hear a well-known and widely-advertised musician singer from New York City. The building was packed. The singer sang with a wonderful natural voice that had been polished by the best training available. After the concert McDaniel said to Frank Cunningham: "Captain, he had a well-modulated voice, with a wide range, but it did not touch my heart. What was the matter?" They reached a brilliant electric light at that moment. Frank Cunningham stopped. Pointing his finger to his heart he replied: "He didn't have it in here. If you haven't got it in here you can't sing." Then, pointing his finger to McDaniel's heart he said: "And you can't preach either."[10]

10. George W. McDaniel, *The Churches of the New Testament* (Nashville: Broadman, 1921), p. 113.

16

Anointed Preaching

In the area of speech communications the gospel preacher has an advantage that separates him from all other public communicators. There is an ingredient that enables the preacher's words to be pointed, sharp, and powerful. This ingredient—anointed preaching—distinguishes gospel preaching from all other methods of communication.

Anointed preaching places God into the sermon and on the preacher. When a preacher preaches in the power of God, the results are remarkable. He preaches with inspiration and fullness of thought. There is both freedom and simplicity of utterance. The results are nothing short of miraculous. This element of the divine in preaching must be foremost in the preacher's preparation and delivery if he is to be lastingly effective. The story is told that once the devil was preaching the gospel. When a saint became alarmed his fears were quieted with the words: "Have no fear; the preaching of the devil will do no good; there is no power in it."[1] No one can preach with power apart from the anointing of the Holy Spirit.

Anointed Preaching in the Bible

Several passages of Scripture indicate the role of the Holy Spirit in gospel preaching. In Matthew 10:19-20 Jesus promises: "But when they deliver you up, take no thought how or what ye

1. W. A. Criswell, *The Holy Spirit in Today's World* (Grand Rapids: Zondervan, 1966), p. 78.

shall speak: for it shall be given you in that same hour what ye shall speak. For it is not ye that speak, but the Spirit of your Father which speaketh in you." First Corinthians 12:3 refers to "speaking by the Spirit of God." Acts 14:3 says that Paul and his party were "speaking boldly in the Lord." We are also told that the Spirit of the Lord even came upon those who listened while the preacher preached. In Acts 11:15 Peter testifies to this fact: "And as I began to speak, the Holy Ghost fell on them, as on us at the beginning."

The words of Paul in 1 Corinthians 2:1-5 are classic in this connection. They set forth with great clarity Paul's understanding of the role of the Holy Spirit in preaching. He begins by saying that he did not come to the Corinthian believers with "excellency of speech or of wisdom, declaring. . .the testimony of God." In those days the Greek orators were famous for their eloquence and rhetorical display. Beyond question Paul was well trained and quite capable of eloquence. Yet he indicates he made no effort to speak in this manner. There is the danger that the naturally gifted preacher will try to use his own eloquence to get the message over. The result may be that he so adorns what he says that he says nothing at all. Thomas Carlisle, hearing a very eloquent man, said: "If that man had anything to say, he could really say it!"

In 1 Corinthians 2:4 Paul continues by saying: "And my speech and my preaching was not with enticing words of man's wisdom, but in demonstration of the Spirit and of power." Corinthian speakers were well-known for their persuasive words and powers of poetic expression. They were spellbinders. They could mesmerize their listeners with their learning and oratorical skills. The preacher may impress his listeners with his logic and skill but actually leave them unmoved at the deepest level of their existence. Paul makes it emphatically clear that the success of preaching and effective sermon delivery does not depend upon the skill of the preacher. This is not to say that we cannot yield gifts of speech to be used by the Lord. But preaching, to be genuinely effective, must be in the demonstration of the Spirit's power. Such preaching produces a spiritual power with results that are unassailable. When Paul preached, miraculous things happened!

Thus the Christian has a power of communication available to him that is not available to other speakers. The Holy Spirit conveys the message to the heart. One word spoken in the power of the Holy Spirit can stab the human heart and change it forever.

What Anointed Preaching Does

Spirit-anointed preaching does something for the preacher. When he preaches in the power of the Spirit he is aware of a power not his own. In the best sense of the word, he is "possessed." He is caught up in the message by the power of the Spirit. He becomes a channel. The Holy Spirit uses him. Every true preacher of the gospel earnestly desires this anointing upon his preaching. It is the ingredient that really makes him a preacher. When D. L. Moody was filled with the Holy Spirit he continued to preach the same sermon outlines he had used before. But there was a distinct difference in his sermons. Something had happened. God was upon them and on him.

Spirit-anointed preaching also does something to the people. The people are gripped, moved, convicted. When the Holy Spirit takes over in the preaching event something miraculous happens. Dr. R. G. Lee, for many years pastor of Bellevue Baptist Church, Memphis, Tennessee, relates such an experience. It took place on a Sunday in 1955. About that morning Dr. Lee said: "It seemed as though Someone had wrapped a warm blanket about me. There was a sensation as though Someone's tender fingertips were caressing me, up and down my body." Never before had Dr. Lee experienced such a mysterious feeling. He said to a person he saw that morning: "There is going to be a great day at Bellevue today." During the service Dr. Lee preached a brief sermon—something unusual for him to do. His text was simple: "And he brought him to Jesus" (John 1:42). He spoke simply, with quiet intensity, and with directness. When the sermon was over the whole congregation was under the spell of the power of God. The invitation was given. The people started to come. The service was not concluded until 12:45 P.M. The whole congregation was visibly moved. People streamed down the aisle. When the day was over 126 persons had made some kind of decision. That evening Dr. Lee baptized 52 new converts as a result of the morning's service. Dr. Lee said: "Nobody can go through a day like this and doubt the reality of the Holy Spirit and His work in convicting people of sin, of righteousness, and of judgment. The movement among people today was as when, in Ezekiel's day, the Valley of Dry Bones became a living army."[2]

When asked to give a definition of anointed preaching, a country preacher scratched his head and replied: "I don't know exactly what it is; but I sure know what it ain't!" Jesus said: "The Spirit of the Lord is upon me, because he hath anointed me to preach the gospel" (Luke 4:18). Anointed preaching is the power of the Holy Spirit upon the man of God as he preaches. This anointing is the ultimate source of preaching power and the true secret of effective sermon delivery.

The Only Effective Preaching

Preaching is effective only when it is accompanied by the Holy Spirit's power. In preaching actually two are involved, for there must be cooperation between the Spirit of God and the man of God. An awareness of this partnership brings about confidence and assurance as the preacher stands to preach. The same power that anointed the preachers of the New Testament is at the disposal of every sincere preacher of the gospel. He must only open himself to the filling of the Holy Spirit for preaching power.

A serious contemplation of the responsibilities of preaching can be overwhelming. Every sincere preacher is aware of his own weakness and finiteness. He must say with Paul that he has this treasure in jars of clay (2 Cor. 4:7). Only as the Holy Spirit comes upon him can he even dare to attempt his high and noble calling. Charles Spurgeon talked about his weekly preaching in the Metropolitan Tabernacle. Fifteen steps led up to the pulpit. It is said that as Spurgeon mounted those stairs with slow,

2. John E. Huss, *Robert G. Lee* (New York: Macmillan, 1948), pp. 196-201.

methodical steps he muttered to himself at each step: "I believe in the Holy Ghost."[3]

If you have preached for any period of time, you have experienced preaching both with and without the power of the Holy Spirit. When the Holy Spirit anoints you to preach there is power and blessing. When you preach in your own strength and skill, there is nothing. On occasion I have decided to preach a sermon I have previously used. When preached at other times the sermon was preached well and produced good results. However, this time things were different. The sermon did not preach well at all. There was little or no response. What made the difference? When the sermon was blessed the Holy Spirit came upon me and gave me unction to preach. Without the Spirit's blessing upon the sermon, it was not much of a message. There is nothing as exhilarating as preaching when the Spirit's anointing is evident. The message soars, words come easily, and the desired results occur. But when he preaches in his own strength, the preacher finds nothing harder or more frustrating.

By Holy Spirit-anointed preaching I do not mean mere emotion or noise. I mean the Holy Spirit's coming upon you in a special manner, providing an abundance of power. The Old Testament prophets had this anointing. The New Testament preachers were anointed to preach. This anointing is not something that happens one time and remains upon the preacher forever. This anointing must be sought every time you preach.

How to Obtain Anointing for Preaching

There are several prerequisites to obtaining the Spirit's anointing. The preacher must be a genuinely born-again man who has an intimate relationship with the Lord Jesus. More than one preacher has preached several years only to discover that he was preaching a message he had never himself experienced. Be sure of your own personal relationship with Jesus Christ.

The life must be clean if the Spirit is to come upon you. The Bible says: "Be ye clean, that bear the vessels of the Lord" (Isa.

3. John R. W. Stott, *Between Two Worlds* (Grand Rapids: Eerdmans, 1982), p. 334.

52:11). God's Holy Spirit will not come upon an uncleansed, unsanctified life. Never go into the pulpit without earnestly praying that you will be emptied of all sin and self. We want our lives to be clean so that the Lord can flow freely through us.

If the Holy Spirit is to come upon us in great power, we must maintain a definite Bible study and prayer life. No preacher can be effectively used of the Holy Spirit apart from a daily time with God. Spend time alone before the Lord. Let your sermon become a sacrifice. The great Athenian statesman, Pericles, often said that so solemn did he deem the act of speaking, he could not begin without an anxious invocation to the immortal gods for their assistance. Surely the gospel preacher should approach the sacred pulpit with as much prayerfulness as would Pericles.

To preach a sermon is a great and awesome task. Pity the man who approaches such a holy calling with poor preparation and a prayerless heart. E. M. Bounds says: "The preacher who has never learned in the school of Christ the high and divine act of intercession for his people will never learn the art of preaching, though homiletics be poured into him by the ton, and though he be the most gifted genius in sermon-making and sermon-delivery."[4]

How to Recognize Anointed Preaching

How may we tell when the anointing of the Holy Spirit is upon our sermon delivery? The preacher is aware of this anointing in his own inmost being. As he preaches he is cognizant that he is a man possessed. The Lord takes a hold of him and uses him. When the anointing of the Spirit of God is upon your preaching you know in your spirit that God is at work. The people are aware of anointed preaching as well. The difference is immediate and dramatic. They are gripped by what is said. Conviction, a deep sense of God's presence, and moving of heart are theirs.

We must seek the Spirit's anointing. Ask Him to come upon

---

4. E. M. Bounds, *Power Through Prayer* (London: Marshall, Morgan and Scott, n.d.), p. 102.

you and your message. Allow Him to manifest His power in and through you. Never be satisfied with anything less in your sermon delivery. You may not always experience the power of the Holy Spirit upon your preaching in equal measure. For reasons in the realm of the mysterious, there are times when the anointing of the Spirit comes upon us in larger measure than at other times. That is beyond question. But there should be such surrender of life to the Spirit that every time we preach there is the evidence of God's blessing upon us.

A Personal Experience

In closing this chapter I would like to share with you an experience I had in preaching that illustrates what I am trying to say in this chapter. In 1977 I was assigned the responsibility to preach at the Alabama Baptist State Evangelism Conference. This conference was held in the church I served as pastor, Dauphin Way Baptist Church, Mobile, Alabama. Several months prior to the meeting I had a definite impression from the Lord to speak on the subject of the Ascension of Jesus Christ. I started gathering material. I studied every passage in the Bible that dealt with the theme of our Lord's ascension. I found every bit of information I could on this subject. I read every sermon I could find on the subject. I exhausted every possible resource in preparing this message. Within a month of the time I was to deliver this message I became aware that God was working in my heart and life in a peculiar way. The theme consumed me. I could hardly stay away from my study. Many nights I stayed up into the wee hours studying and preparing this message. Many, many times God's presence was so overwhelming as I prepared I would actually weep.

The day came for me to deliver the message. The conference to that point had been average. Nothing unusual seemed to be happening. There was no evidence that anything unusual was going to take place. I approached my assignment with great fear and trepidation. I almost had a sense of dread. But when I began to preach, something happened. Barely five minutes into the message the Spirit of God seemed to take complete possession of me. The congregation of mostly preachers was caught up as well. I felt as if I were actually in another world. There were times throughout the message when I did actually feel as if I were an onlooker, rather than the preacher for the occasion. Never, before nor since, have I been so stirred and moved by the Holy Spirit.

The Lord blessed the delivery of my message "Our Ascended Lord." The conference of preachers seemed to be swept along in a floodtide of joy and spiritual excitement. When the message was over we were all aware that God had visited us. In the days and weeks just after I preached, the tapes literally swept the nation. They were sent into every state of the union and many, many foreign countries. When preachers heard the tape in distant places the same spiritual phenomenon occurred. Phone calls and letters began to pour in. Preachers at the point of despair were lifted and encouraged by the message. I knew I was not responsible for the results.

Almost eight years have passed since that memorable day. There has hardly been a week since that I have not heard from someone who has been blessed by the message. What is the secret of its power? Why has there been such unusual blessing as a result of it? I have listened to the tape of the message numerous times. There are many, many flaws in it. The delivery is far from the standards I have advised in this book. I see many ways in which the message could have been delivered more effectively from rhetorical and psychological points of view. I have only one explanation for the results and effectiveness of the message. The Holy Spirit of God anointed me in a special way on a special occasion for a special task. I really had little to do with the delivery of the message. The message was delivered through me by the Holy Spirit.

I wish that every sermon I deliver could be accompanied with a similar evidence of the Spirit's power. Perhaps my own humanness prevents this from being possible. I do know, however, that such anointing with the Spirit's power is the desire and goal of every preacher assigned the glorious responsibility of delivering the Word of God to men. Seek the anointing of the Spirit.

Conclusion

Writing this book has been a personal matter to me. Actually it is the climax of several years of personal study in the area of sermon delivery. In the process of working on my own delivery this book has been conceived and born. I do not present its contents from the viewpoint of an expert on the subject. I am constantly aware of my own need for additional work, study, and improvement in delivery. My hope is that I may be able to help my fellow preachers who are involved weekly in delivering sermons. Perhaps this book will help both you and me become more effective communicators of the Word of God.

Reading this book will not be a wonder drug for your delivery. You may master the basic contents of what I have said, yet you will never get to the point that you will not need additional study and improvement. There will be days when you will struggle in the delivery of your message. You will move with the difficulty of the snail. On other days, you will soar like an eagle. The words will flow, the ingredients of effective sermon delivery will come together in a powerful combination, and you will preach the stars down. If this book can make the latter experience occur more often, I will be grateful.

My desire is that this book will get you started toward a lifetime of study in the area of sermon delivery. Let me encourage you to study all aspects of delivery. Keep abreast of the latest information in the field. Several areas of the preaching dynamic I have touched upon in this work need additional research and study by those who are experts in the field. Listen to good speakers and preachers. Learn from them. Benefit from their strengths. Avoid their mistakes.

Listen to yourself. See that every sermon you preach is taped. Listen to it carefully. Correct your mistakes during practice sessions. Learn from them. Ask yourself, Why was this not effective? Ask, How could I have said that better?

The only way to learn to preach is to preach. I agree that preaching is an art. There must be practice, practice, then more practice. But merely preaching week by week is not sufficient. Preaching weekly may be compared to the carpenter who weekly plies his trade. If he does not develop and sharpen his skills of carpentry, he may weekly repeat the same mistakes. Likewise, the preacher must engage in *meaningful* practice. He must carefully observe his strengths and his weaknesses. He must develop and improve his preaching skills.

Do not allow sermon delivery to become an obsession to you. You can become so concerned about the details of delivery that you actually bind yourself and make it difficult to preach. I emphasize again: Do your practicing outside the pulpit. The benefits of your practice will naturally transfer into your pulpit delivery. I like the approach of the black preacher who summed up his preparation this way: "First, I reads myself full, next I thinks myself clear, and next I prays myself hot, and then I lets go."[1]

Preach Jesus, and you will always have an audience. St. Bernard said: "Yesterday, I preached myself, and the scholars came up and praised me. Today, I preached Christ, and the sinners came up and thanked me." Make a full surrender of yourself to preach Jesus and His wonderful Word. Then, as you stand to preach, God will wonderfully bless you as you "lift up your voice!"

1. In John R. W. Stott, *Between Two Worlds* (Grand Rapids: Eerdmans, 1982), p. 258.

Selected Bibliography

Adams, Jay. *Pulpit Speech.* Phillipsburg, N.J.: Presbyterian and Reformed, 1971.

_____ . *Sense Appeal in the Sermons of Charles Haddon Spurgeon.* Grand Rapids: Baker, 1975.

Bacon, Wallace A. *The Art of Interpretation.* New York: Holt, Rinehart, and Winston, 1972.

Blackwood, A. W. *Expository Preaching for Today.* Grand Rapids: Baker, 1943.

Bounds, E. M. *Power Through Prayer.* London: Marshall, Morgan and Scott, n.d.

Brigance, William N. *The Use of Words: Speech Composition.* New York: F. S. Crofts, 1937.

Broadus, John A. *The Preparation and Delivery of Sermons.* New York: Harper, 1926.

Brodnitz, Friedrich S. *Keep Your Voice Healthy.* Springfield, Ill.: Thomas, 1973.

Buffington, Perry W. "Psychology of Eyes." *Sky 13,* no. 2 (February 1984):92-96.

Crandell, S. Judson, and Gerald M. Phillips. *Speech: A Course in Fundamentals.* Glenview, Ill.: Scott, Foresman, 1963.

Criswell, W. A. *The Holy Spirit in Today's World.* Grand Rapids: Zondervan, 1966.

Curry, S. S. *Vocal and Literary Interpretation of the Bible.* New York: Doran, 1903.

Dabney, Robert. *Sacred Rhetoric*. Edinburgh: Banner of Truth, 1979.

Demaray, Donald. *An Introduction to Homiletics*. Grand Rapids: Baker, 1974.

Dickens, Milton. *Speech: Dynamic Communication*. New York: Harcourt Brace Jovanovich, 1954.

Eisenson, John. *Voice and Diction*. New York: Macmillan, 1974.

Fairbanks, Grand. *Voice and Articulation Drillbook*. New York: Harper & Row, 1940.

Fasol, Al. "A Guide to Improving Your Preaching Delivery." Southwestern Baptist Theological Seminary, Ft. Worth, Tex. Mimeographed.

Forman, R. C. *Public Speaking Made Easy*. Grand Rapids: Baker, 1967.

Forrest, Mary, and Margot A. Olson, *Exploring Speech Communication*. St. Paul: West, 1981.

Grasham, John A., and Glenn G. Gooder, *Improving Your Speech*. New York: Harcourt, Brace and World, 1960.

Griffin, Emory A. *The Mind Changers*. Wheaton, Ill.: Tyndale, 1976.

Henderson, George. *Lectures to Young Preachers*. Edinburgh: B. McCall Barbour, 1961.

Hoffman, William G. *How to Make Better Speeches*. New York: Funk & Wagnalls, 1976.

Horne, Chevis F. *Dynamic Preaching*. Nashville: Broadman, 1983.

Huss, John E. *Robert G. Lee*. Grand Rapids: Zondervan, 1967.

Jones, Winston E. *Preaching and the Dramatic Arts*. New York: Macmillan, 1948.

King, Robert. *Forms of Public Address*. Indianapolis: Bobbs-Merrill, 1969.

Kirkpatrick, Robert White. *The Creative Delivery of Sermons*. Joplin, Mo.: Joplin College, 1944.

Koller, Charles W. *Expository Preaching Without Notes*. Grand Rapids: Baker, 1962.

Lee, Charlotte I., and Frank Galati. *Oral Interpretation*. Boston: Houghton Mifflin, 1977.

Lloyd-Jones, D. Martyn. *Preaching and Preachers*. Grand Rapids: Zondervan, 1971.

Magoon, E. L. *The Modern Whitefield.* New York: Sheldon, Blakeman, 1856.

McClosky, David Blair. *Your Voice at Its Best.* Plymouth, Mass.: Memorial, 1972.

McDaniel, George W. *The Churches of the New Testament.* Nashville: Broadman, 1921.

McDowell, Josh. "Syllabus on Communication and Persuasion." Josh McDowell, 1983. Mimeographed.

McFarland, Kenneth. *Eloquence in Public Speaking.* Englewood Cliffs, N.J.: Prentice-Hall, 1961.

McKenzie, E. C. *Mac's Great Book of Quips and Quotes.* Grand Rapids: Baker, 1980.

Mulgrave, Dorothy. *Speech.* New York: Barnes and Noble, 1954.

Neal, Anna Lloyd. *A Syllabus for Fundamentals of Speech.* Greenville, S.C.: Bob Jones U., 1977.

Overstreet, H. A. *Influencing Human Behavior.* New York: Norton, 1925.

Prochnow, Herbert V. *Speaker's Handbook of Epigrams and Witticisms.* Grand Rapids: Baker, 1955.

Rahskoph, Horace G. *Basic Speech Improvement.* New York: Harper & Row, 1965.

Reid, Loren. *Speaking Well.* New York: McGraw-Hill, 1977.

Robinson, Haddon W. *Biblical Preaching.* Grand Rapids: Baker, 1980.

Sarnoff, Dorothy. *Speech Can Change Your Life.* New York: Dell, 1970.

Spurgeon, Charles H. *Lectures to My Students.* London: Marshall, Morgan and Scott, 1954.

Stevenson, Dwight E., and Charles F. Diehl. *Reaching People from the Pulpit.* Grand Rapids: Baker, 1958.

Stott, John R. W. *Between Two Worlds.* Grand Rapids: Eerdmans, 1982.

Tan, Paul Lee. *Signs of the Times.* Rockville, Maryland: Assurance, n.d.

Thayer, Joseph Henry. *Greek-English Lexicon.* Grand Rapids: Zondervan, 1963.

Weaver, Richard L. II. *Understanding Interpersonal Communication.* Dallas: Scott, Foresman, 1981.

Whitsell, Farris D. *Power in Expository Preaching.* Old Tappan, N.J.: Revell, 1963.

Wiersbe, Warren W., and David Wiersbe. *Making Sense of the Ministry.* Chicago: Moody, 1983.

Wiersbe, Warren W. *Walking with the Giants.* Grand Rapids: Baker, 1976.